EGYPTIAN ART

ART IN DETAIL

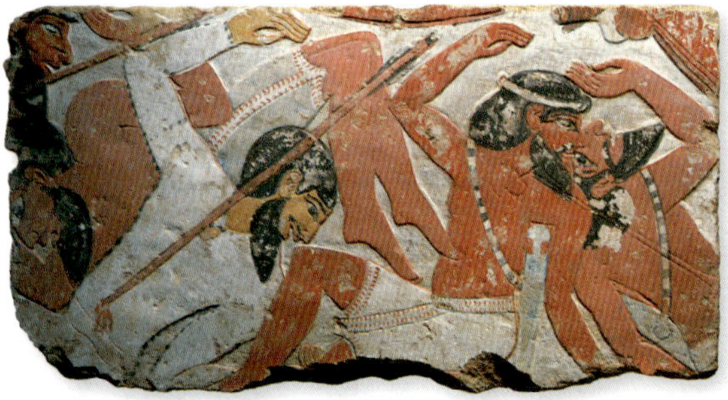

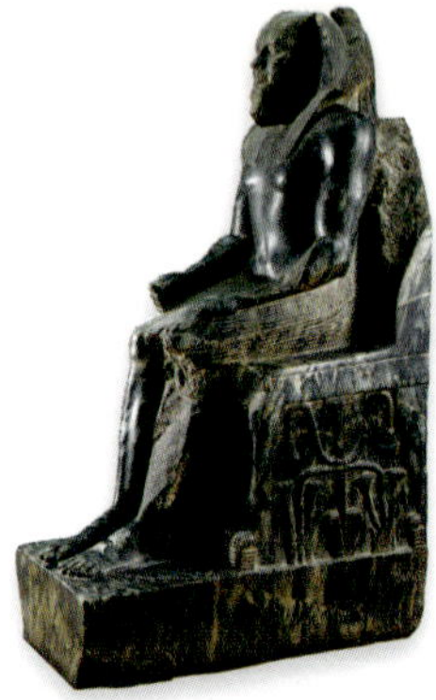

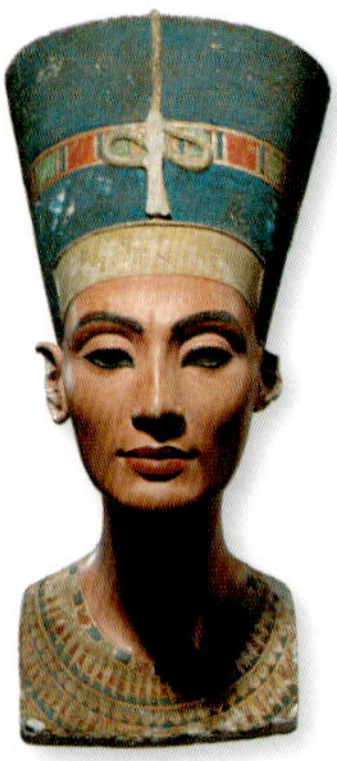

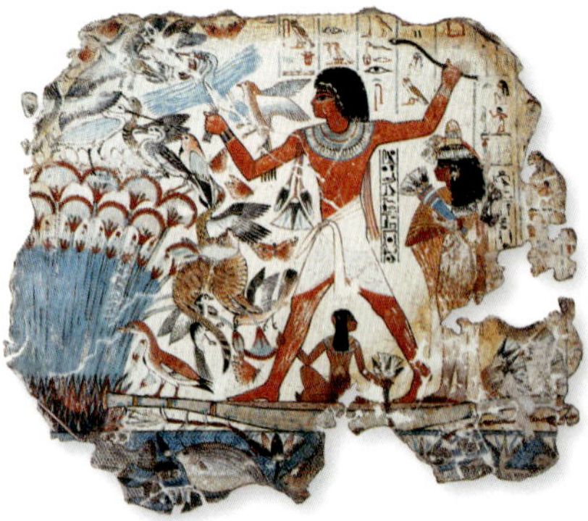

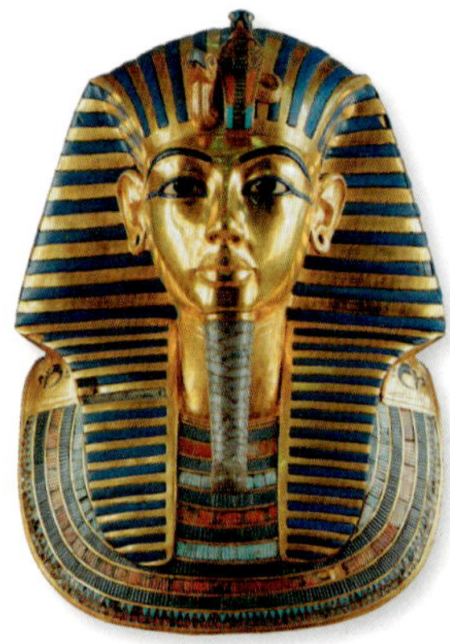

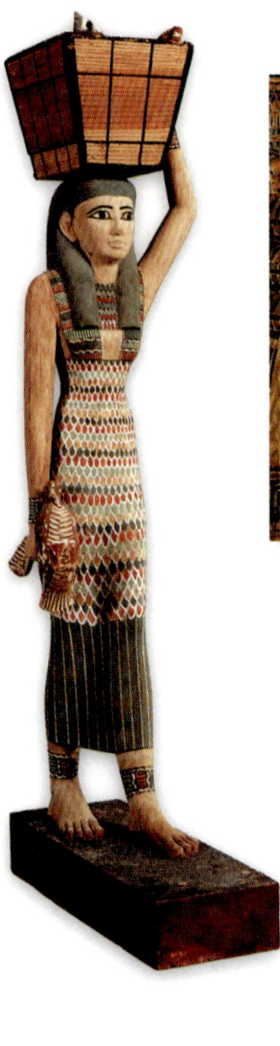

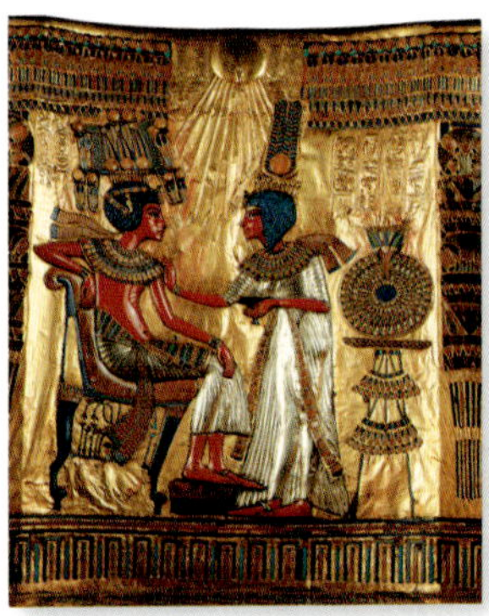

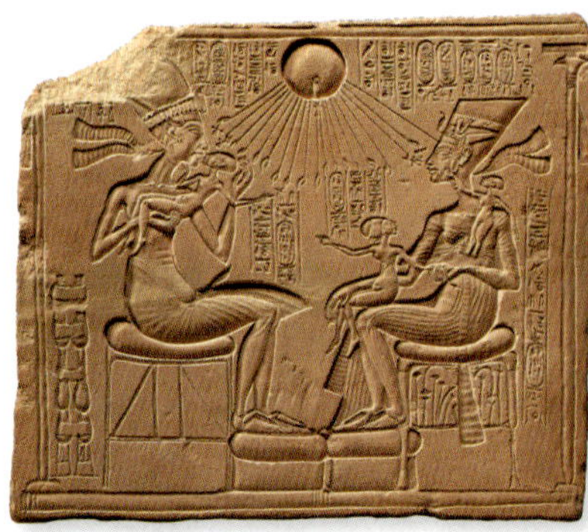

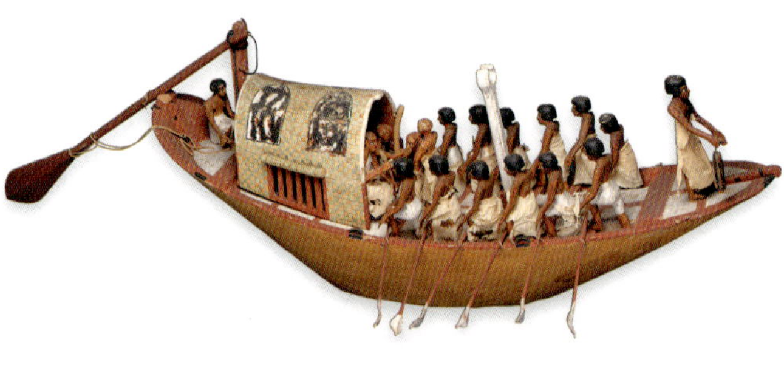

Egyptian Art

Art in Detail

Susie Hodge

METRO BOOKS
NEW YORK

This 2008 edition published by Metro Books,
by arrangement with Ivy Press.

This book was conceived, designed,
and produced by

Ivy Press

The Old Candlemakers
West Street, Lewes,
East Sussex BN7 2NZ, U.K.

Creative Director Peter Bridgewater
Publisher Jason Hook
Editorial Director Caroline Earle
Art Director Clare Harris
Senior Project Editor James Thomas
Designer Jon Raimes
Concept Design Alan Osbahr
Picture Research Katie Greenwood
Consultant Editor Dr. Christina Riggs

Metro Books
122 Fifth Avenue
New York, NY 10011

ISBN-13: 978-1-4351-0380-1
ISBN-10: 1-4351-0380-7

Printed and bound in China

10 9 8 7 6 5 4 3 2 1

Picture Credits
The publisher would like to thank the following for their permission to reproduce the images in this book. Every effort has been made to acknowledge the images, however we apologize if there are any unintentional omissions.

Akg-images/Erich Lessing: 110–105. **Scala, Florence**: 8–13, 62–67, 68–73, 74–79; © Bildarchiv Preussischer Kulturbesitz, Berlin: 44–49, 50–55; © HIP: 32–37, 38–43, 56–61, 80–85, 86–91, 92–97, 98–103; © The Metropolitan Museum of Art/Art Resource: 14–19, 20–25, 26–31, 104–109, 116–121, 122–127.

Cover Image: **Scala, Florence**.

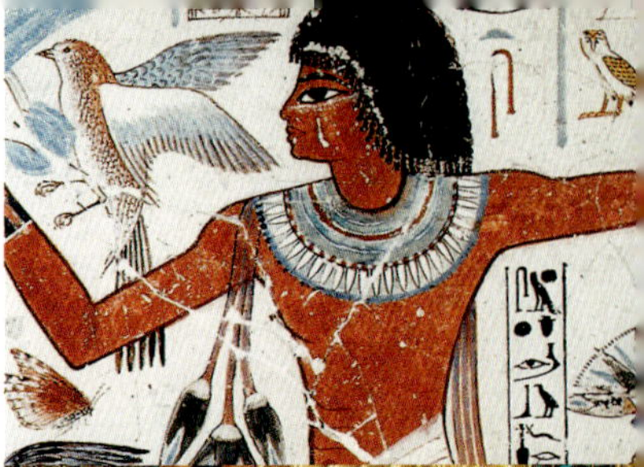

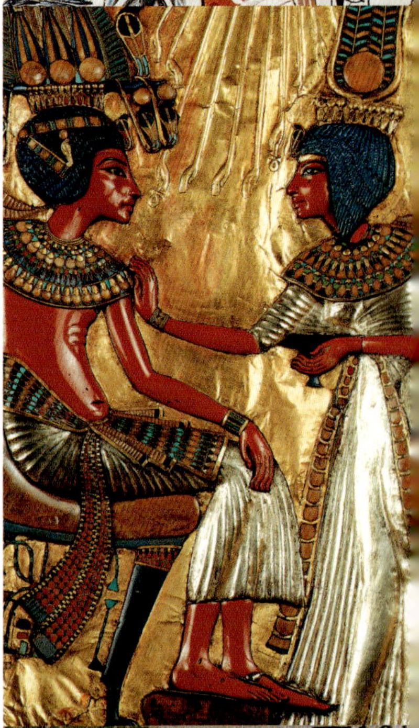

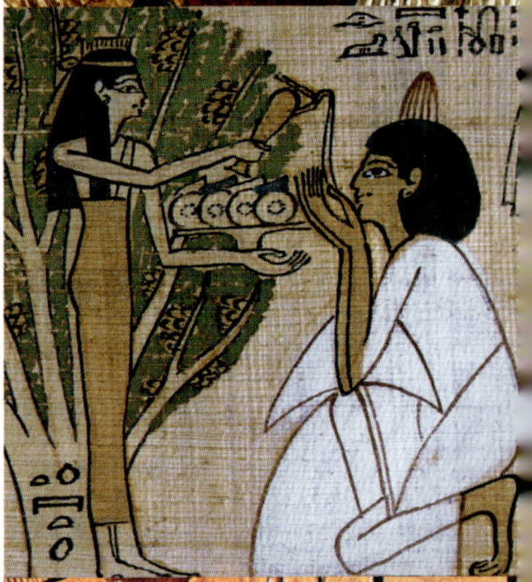

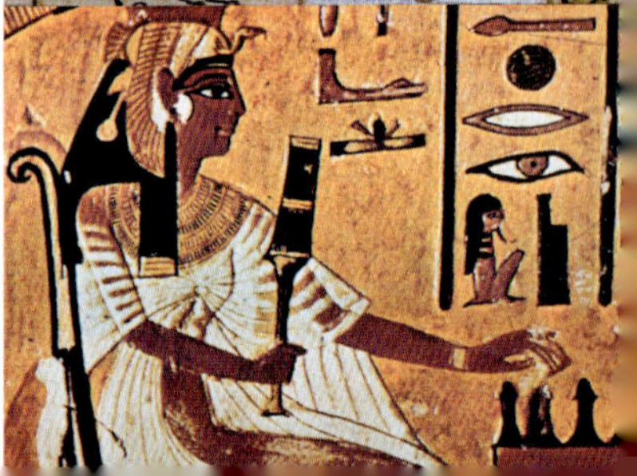

Contents

Introduction

ANCIENT EGYPTIAN ART HAS FASCINATED AND BEGUILED FOR CENTURIES. Coming from the land of blue skies and golden sands, of mysterious rituals, and powerful kings and queens who were revered as gods, the art never seems to lose its charm. Developed by a civilization living in the lower Nile Valley from c.5000 BCE to c.300 BCE, most of the art relates to life after death and was never intended to be seen by humans. Bodies were preserved, pictures painted, sculptures carved—and everything was put where no living person would see it, to make sure that the dead would exist forever. One Egyptian word for sculptor was "He–who–keeps–alive."

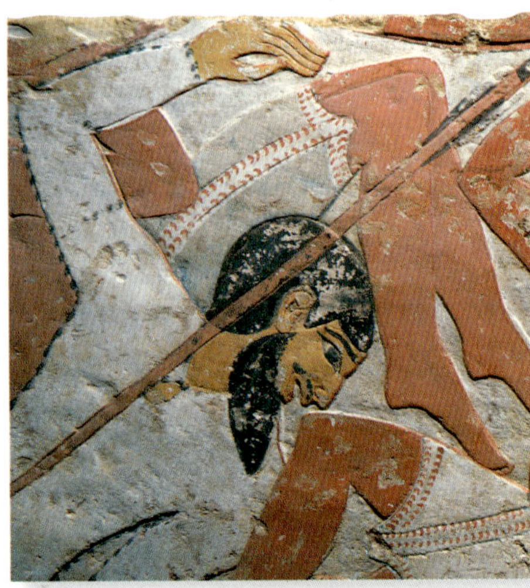

Egypt, like all other ancient civilizations, was deeply influenced by magic, and by a belief in the existence of gods who had to be satisfied if their goodwill was to be secured. As such, most of the art was made as a means of pleasing these gods, meaning that much of it was for the ruling or wealthy classes, although modest artifacts were produced for the ordinary

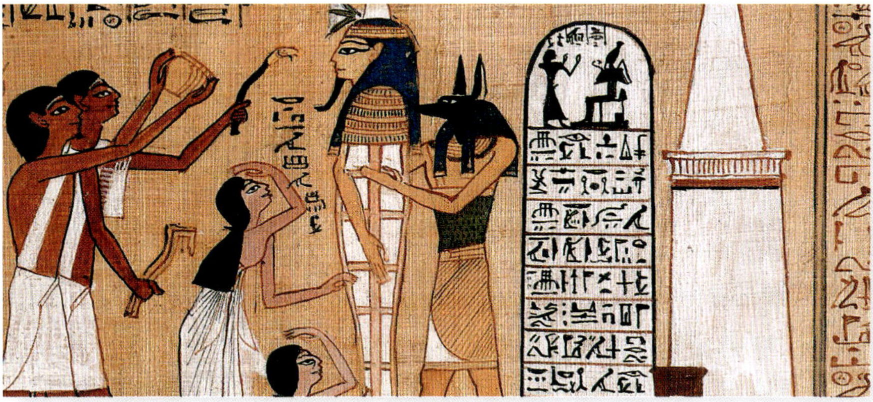

people. With such variety, the art reflects every aspect of the ancient Egyptians' lives, in tomb and temple drawings and paintings, in statues and models, in coffins and containers, and in jewelry made from gold and semiprecious stones. There is a balance and simplicity about the art that has not always been achieved in modern design and, with its keen observation of nature, geometric regularity, and brilliant colors, it crosses the boundaries of fine art and design. Characterized by the idea of order, clean lines combine with simple shapes and flat areas of bright color. The distinctive and harmonious proportions can be seen in everything—from statues and paintings to jewelry and architecture—because the Egyptian concept of space was arranged according to the angles of the sun across the sky, and the flow of the River Nile. This is one of the reasons why, for more than 3,000 years, the art hardly changed.

To choose just 20 works from this rich and diverse culture is not easy. Some recognizable works were essential, so they are here, along with a varied yet representative range, evoking the environments in which they were made. In the light of new excavations and research, the selection also consists of works from royalty, the nobility, and the middle classes, putting some of the most exciting creations in history into context.

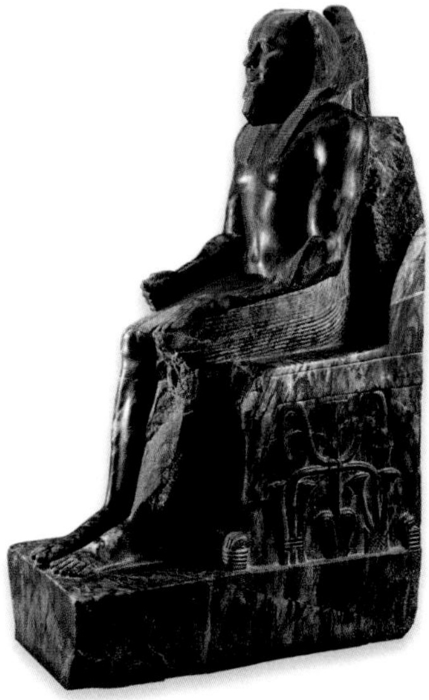

FROM THE VALLEY TEMPLE OF THE PYRAMID OF KHAFRE AT GIZA, NOW IN THE EGYPTIAN MUSEUM, CAIRO

Statue of Khafre Seated

Diorite, 4th dynasty of the Old Kingdom, 2520–2492 BCE

ANCIENT EGYPTIAN HISTORY falls into three main periods, further divided into dynasties (when a single family provided the succession of rulers). The Old Kingdom was the first major period, beginning with the amalgamation of Upper and Lower Egypt and ending with civil war. Order was restored initially during the Middle Kingdom, but it too ended with civil war. Thebes became the main center for the New Kingdom, the period that brought Egypt to its greatest power.

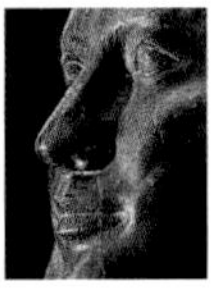

2770 BCE

Egypt introduces 365-day calendar. Its previous calendar was based on the moon's cycle and the stars

2575–2467 BCE

4th dynasty, the "golden age of peace;" the first religious words are written on the walls of royal tombs

c.2560 BCE

First and largest Great Pyramid is built by Khafre's father, Khufu

Artists and craftsmen trained from a young age to learn the rules of art that were imposed to facilitate a smooth transition to the afterlife. The artists' task was to preserve everything as clearly and permanently as possible, so they did not set out to sketch nature as it appeared, but to represent the world as it could most clearly be described, and every artist adhered by these rigorous laws. In addition to large burial monuments, sculptors became proficient at portraiture, frequently combining human and godlike attributes and symbols. Sculpture of the Old Kingdom was characterized by symmetry and solidity.

Khafre, the son of King Khufu and Queen Henutsen, succeeded his half-brother Djedefre and ruled Egypt for approximately 30 years. His reign was one of great splendor. When he built the second pyramid of three at Giza, numerous portrait statues were placed in both his valley temple and his pyramid temple to furnish the rituals that were performed there. "Ka" statues were popular forms of portraiture. They were portraits of important people like the pharaoh, built to adorn that person's burial tomb. If the deceased's mummy was destroyed, ka statues could serve as an abode for the soul in the next world. For this reason, permanence of style and material was essential and some form of stone was usually used. This ka statue of Khafre is one of the original 23 from his tomb at Giza. One of the rules of sculpture was that seated statues had to have their hands on their knees and this one, created by an unknown artist, is of a basic standard design employed by sculptors of the Old Kingdom.

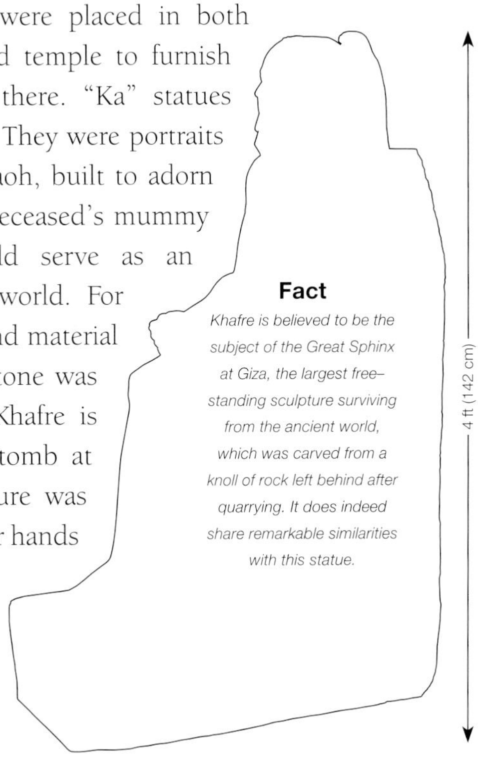

Fact

Khafre is believed to be the subject of the Great Sphinx at Giza, the largest free-standing sculpture surviving from the ancient world, which was carved from a knoll of rock left behind after quarrying. It does indeed share remarkable similarities with this statue.

c.2555–2532 BCE

The Great Pyramids are built in Giza by three different pharaohs

c.2520 BCE

Khafre's pyramid is smaller than Khufu's, but built at a higher level

c.2520–2494 BCE

The Sphinx is built; the largest single-stone statue in the world

2686–2181 BCE

Hieroglyphs become standardized so that all symbols have set meanings and all artists learn them

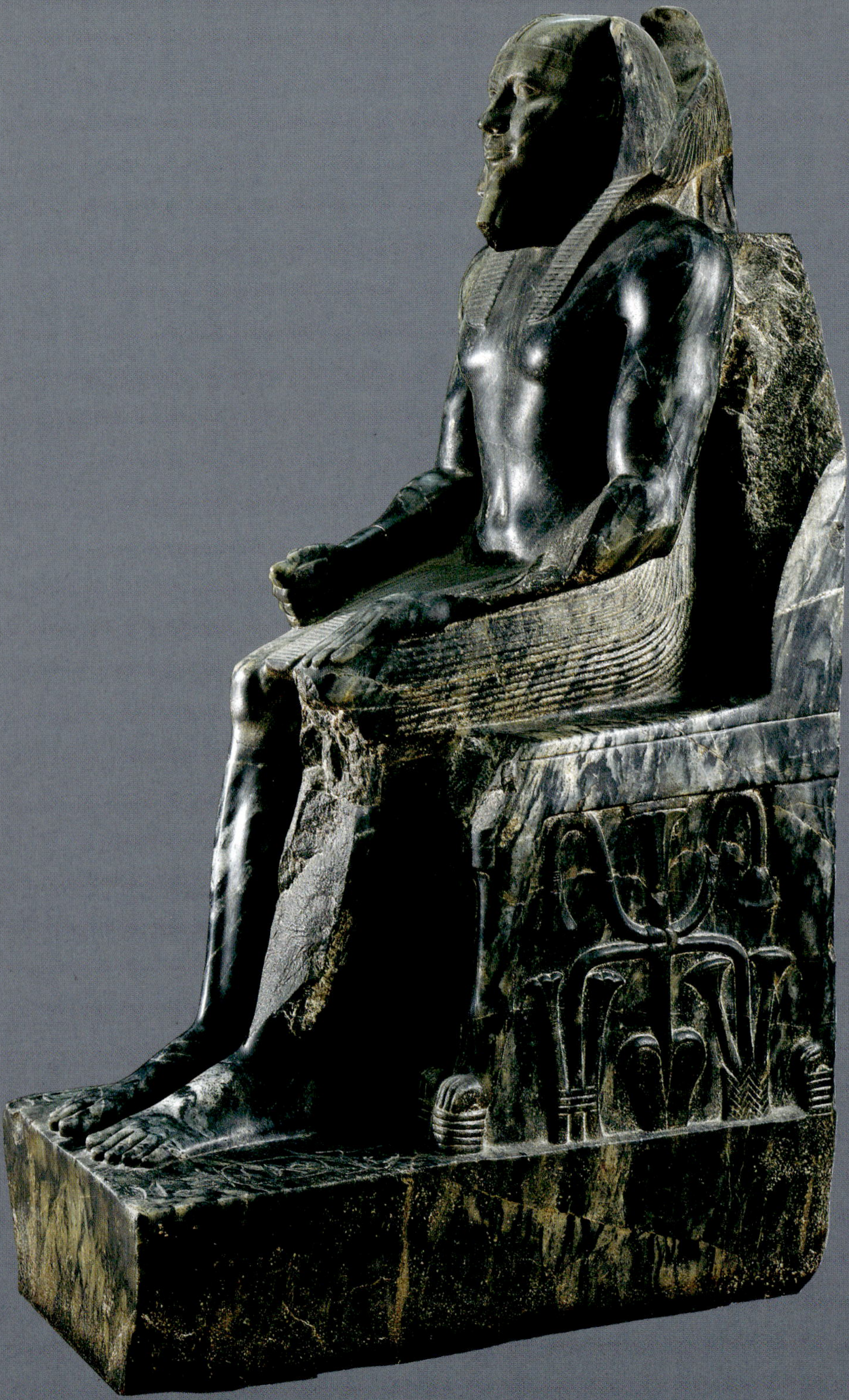

All Khafre's funerary statues are composed in the same basic way. He sits on a square-shape throne with the *sema-tawi*, an emblem of unification that combines the hieroglyph *sema* ("union") with the symbols for the two lands of Egypt—papyrus for the north and a lotus flower for the south. The stems of the plants are knotted around a hieroglyph signifying "to unite," so the throne proclaims Khafre as pharaoh of two lands. Khafre wears a simple kilt and sits rigidly upright on the throne. The falcon god Horus extends his protective wings to shelter the pharaoh's head. Khafre has the royal false beard fastened to his chin and wears the royal linen headdress with the cobra of kingship on his forehead.

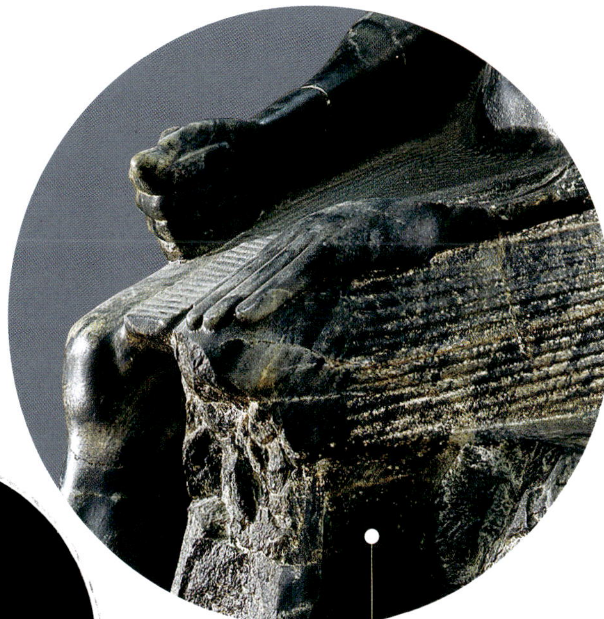

Demonstrating his expertise, the artist created a naturalistic yet idealized statue, dressed in the traditional false beard and linen headdress of the pharaoh.

Khafre's arms, thighs, and his legs are close together and connected to the throne by the stone the artist chose to leave intact.

Khafre is attached to the solid slab that forms the back of his throne. His pose is frontal, rigid, and symmetrical.

The sculptors' purpose was not to record individual features or the distinctive shapes of bodies, but rather to proclaim the godlike nature of Egyptian kingship. By giving the figure compactness and solidity, the form manifests the purpose: to last for eternity.

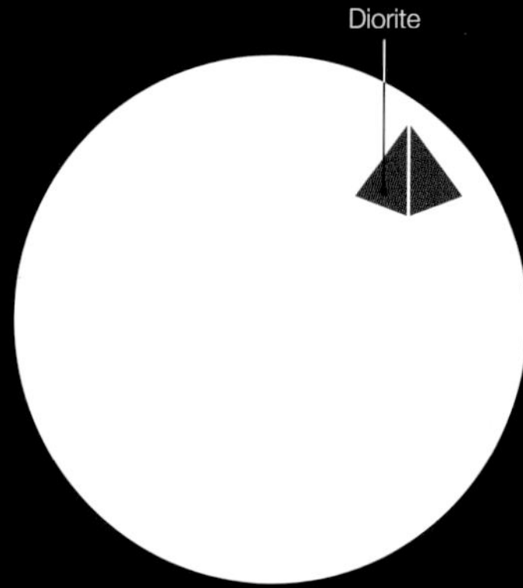

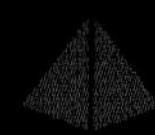

This is the *sema-tawi*, an emblem of the unification of Upper and Lower Egypt. It combines the hieroglyph *sema* (meaning "union") with the symbols for the two lands of Egypt—papyrus for the north and a lotus flower for the south.

Most of the other portrait statues found in Khafre's tomb were damaged and incomplete, but this one was largely intact. Some modern restorations were made on the right side of the torso based on fragments from other statues. The primary material is diorite, a dark greenish-gray, durable stone that was polished to a smooth, rich sheen. This exceptionally hard, dark stone was brought about 400 miles down the Nile from royal quarries in the south. The Egyptians considered idealized proportions essential for representing imposing majesty and applied them even though this was not how the king really looked. These and all other depictions of the pharaohs are not true portraits. The statue presents an archetype of ideal, godlike beauty, worthy of respect and admiration.

According to Egyptian mythology, pharaohs were the sons of gods. Deliberately, the figure of Khafre has no projecting limbs or easily breakable parts. The sculptor produced the statue by first drawing the front, back, and two profile views of the pharaoh on the four vertical faces of the stone block. Once the basic block had been prepared, apprentices chiseled away excess stone on each side, working inward until the planes met at right angles and then rounding the corners. Finally, the master sculpted detailed parts of the face and body. This subtractive method of creating the portrait explains the blocklike look of the statue. This form of carving and creating statues was usual during Khafre's reign, and is also apparent in later dynasties.

The finishing of the statue was done by abrasion (rubbing or grinding the surface with stones and fine sand pastes).

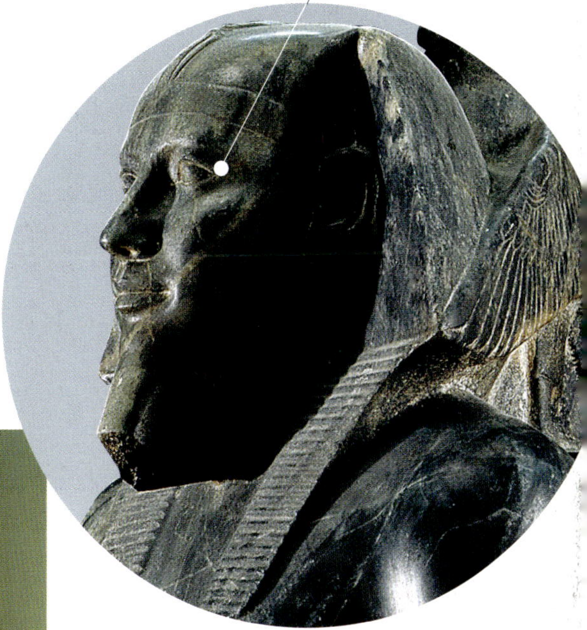

Mummifying bodies was not enough. By preserving the pharaoh's likeness in a painting or statue, he would be doubly sure of existing forever. This was part of the reason why craftsmen strove to attain such perfection—to provide a reserve dwelling place for the pharaoh in the afterlife.

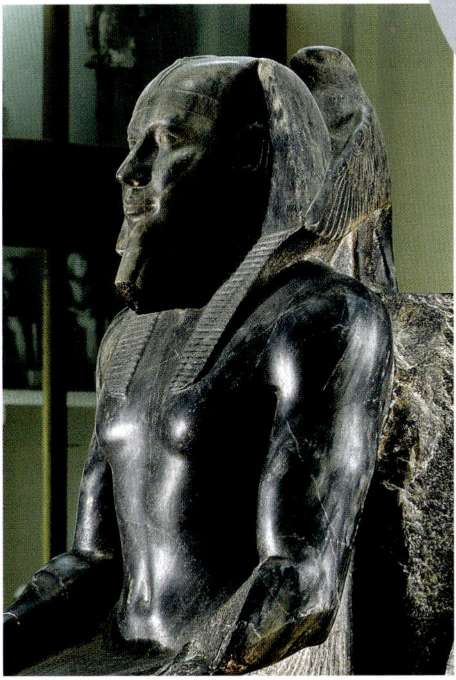

Diorite is an extremely hard stone and extraordinarily difficult to sculpture. Diorite balls were made to grind down hard granites.

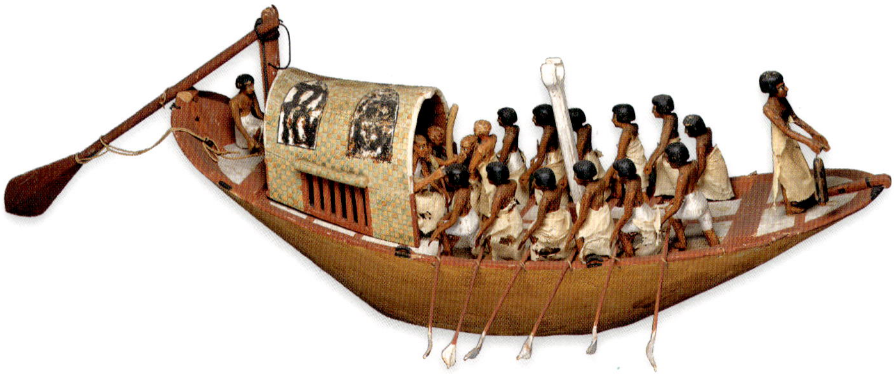

FROM THE TOMB OF MEKETRE, NEAR DEIR EL-BAHRI, NOW IN THE METROPOLITAN MUSEUM OF ART, NEW YORK

Model of a Riverboat

Gesso and painted wood, linen twine, linen, c.1985 BCE

BY THE TIME OF THE MIDDLE KINGDOM, the center of the Upper Egyptian administration was Thebes. Meketre was the chancellor of Mentuhotep II, the 11th dynasty king of the Middle Kingdom and, as a powerful official, was entitled to burial in a rock-cut tomb near Thebes. Although the tomb had collapsed and already been looted when it was discovered in 1920, one chamber still contained a considerable collection of small wooden models like this one, showing various aspects of Meketre's life. This boat and more than 20 other models of boats, gardens, people spinning and weaving, a carpenter's shop, a granary, a bakery, other workshops, and cattle being counted were found in the small burial chamber.

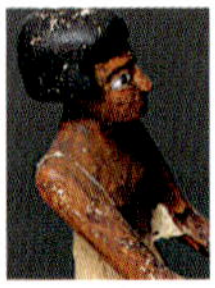

2140–2134 BCE

The First Intermediate Period takes over from the Old Kingdom

2140–1640 BCE

11th dynasty is the first family rule of the Middle Kingdom

c.2065–1998 BCE

Pharaohs order art in the style of the 5th and 6th dynasties—to suggest continuity with earlier rulers

Meketre commissioned the models for his tomb to assist his passage to the next world. In life, he served successive kings from the 11th to the 12th dynasty and, for his services, he was given 10 boats, six for work and four for his personal travel. Virtually all Egyptian traffic traveled on the Nile, so wealthy nobles had their own fleets. This model illustrates a riverboat he had for personal use. Since boats were the chief form of transport in Egypt, models of boats with various functions were considered necessary for the afterlife so, with 15 crew members to transport Meketre safely, the boat is a small copy of one he used in his lifetime. In the same way that wall paintings were painted for other Egyptian nobles, these models were intended to help Meketre travel to the afterlife. Both types of representation showed how the deceased person lived during his or her life on earth. These forms of art also included symbolism that the Egyptians understood and believed the gods would recognize. The blind harpist and singer were known in Egyptian stories for performing songs about the transience of life, which is why they appear here. While some models made during the Middle Kingdom were offerings to the gods and others were children's toys, this model and others in the same tomb were intended purely to accompany Meketre on his final journey and to enrich his life in the next world.

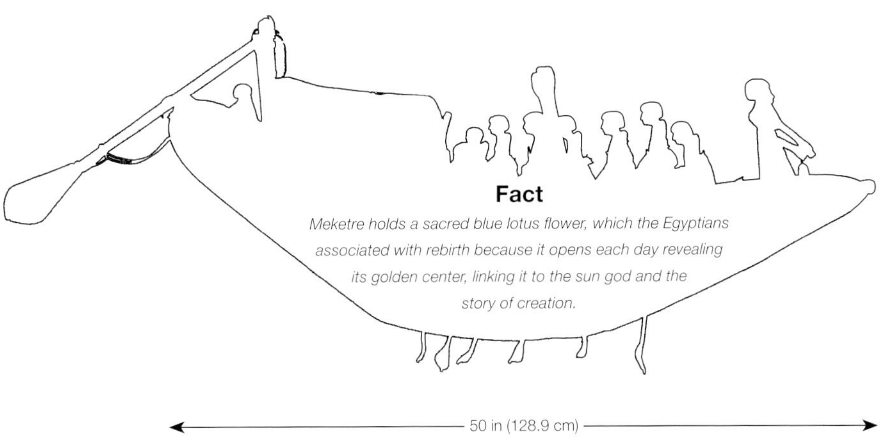

Fact

Meketre holds a sacred blue lotus flower, which the Egyptians associated with rebirth because it opens each day revealing its golden center, linking it to the sun god and the story of creation.

2010-1998 BCE

Mentuhotep II rules both Upper and Lower Egypt

c.2000 BCE

Coffins decorated even more than earlier dynastic styles

c.2000 BCE

Assured, restrained style of wood carving with delicate painting becomes popular

1991–1783 BCE

During the 12th dynasty of the Middle Kingdom, kings build extensively throughout Egypt

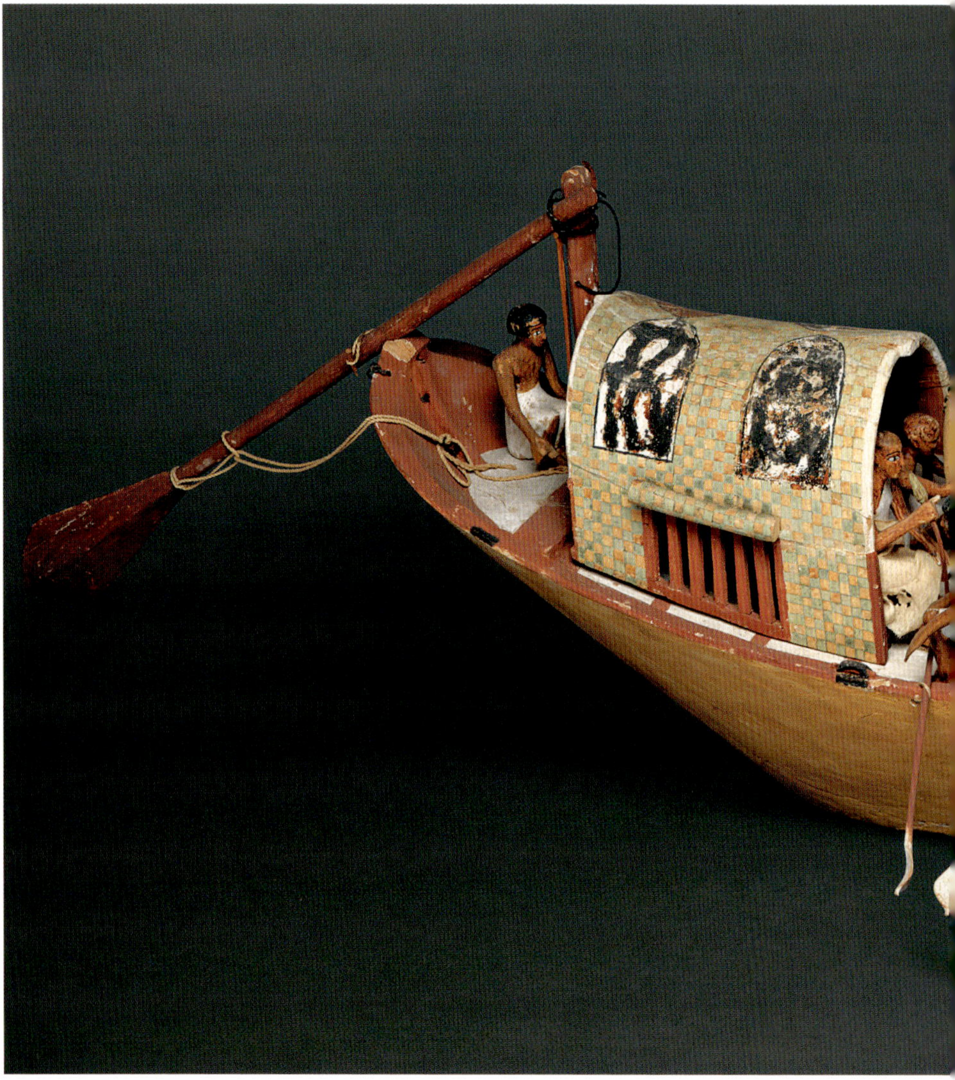

Standing in front of the harpist and singer is the ship's captain, with his arms in front of his body. He may be awaiting orders or he could be paying homage to the deceased Meketre. The 12 oarsmen propel the boat, taking their orders from the captain. At the stern, the helmsman controls the rudder. Meketre sits in the shade of a small cabin, which on an actual boat would have been made of a light wooden framework with linen or leather hangings. Wooden shields covered with bulls' hides are painted on each side of the roof. A tall white post in the center of the boat would have supported a mast and sail, although these have disappeared and were not found in the tomb. They would have been taken down when the boat was rowed downstream against the prevailing north wind and unfurled when the boat was sailing in the opposite direction.

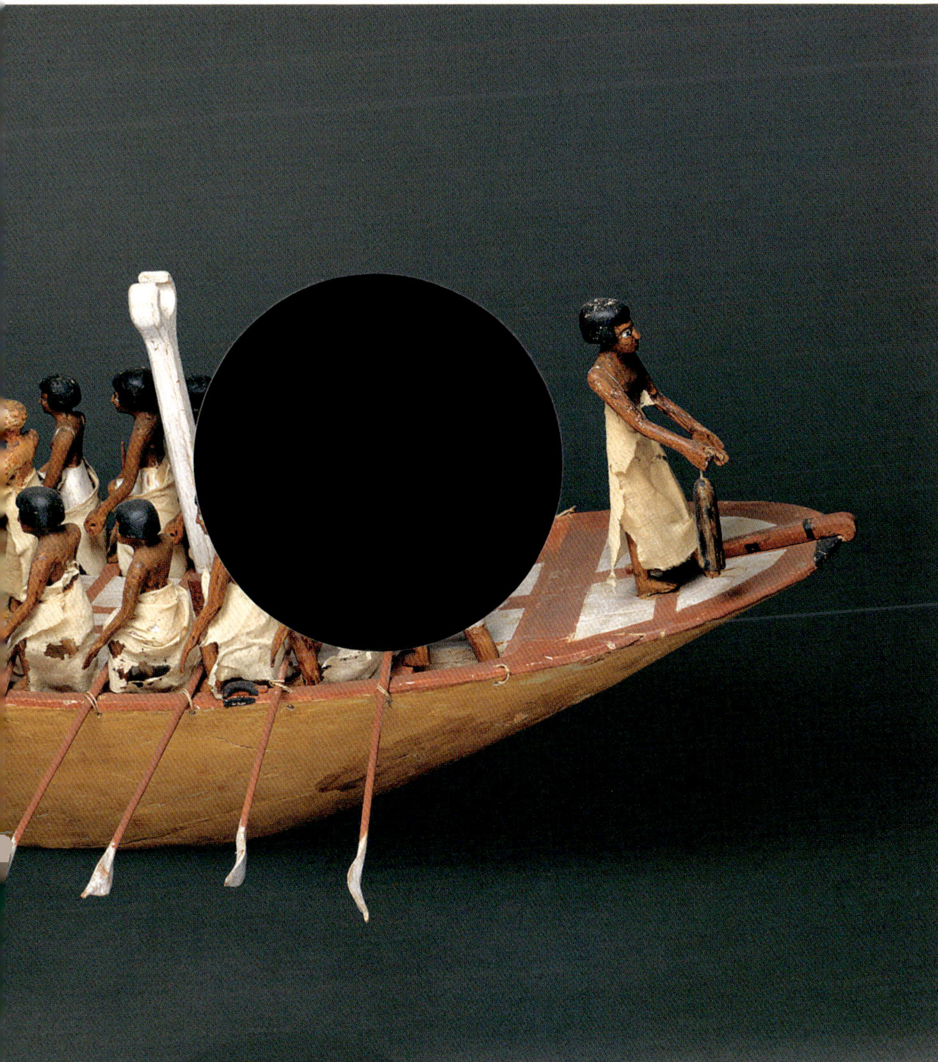

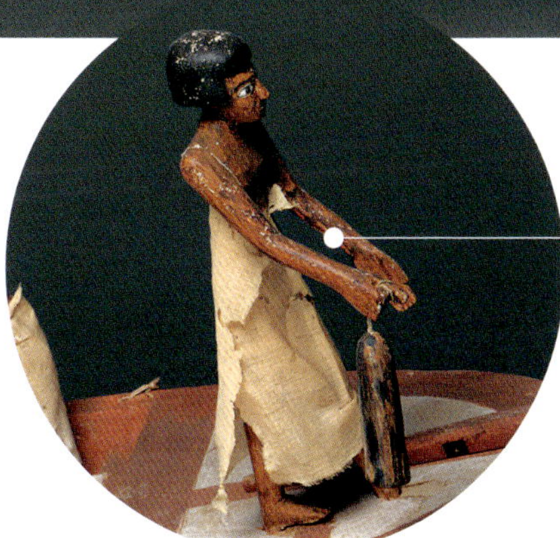

During the New Kingdom, boats were steered by helmsmen holding the rudder in both hands. One helmsman was described like this: "His arms were strong and didn't get tired steering in the stern of the boat."

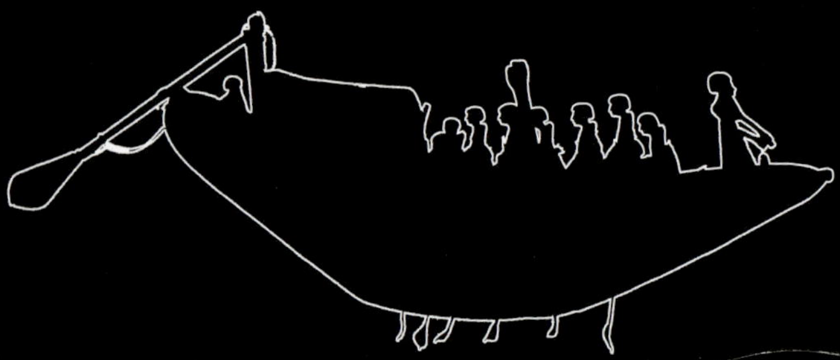

Once the model had been carved and smoothed, the artist applied gesso. This was a mixture of plaster, glue, and water, used as a surface for painting or as a base for low relief. It smoothed the surface of the wood in preparation for the paint.

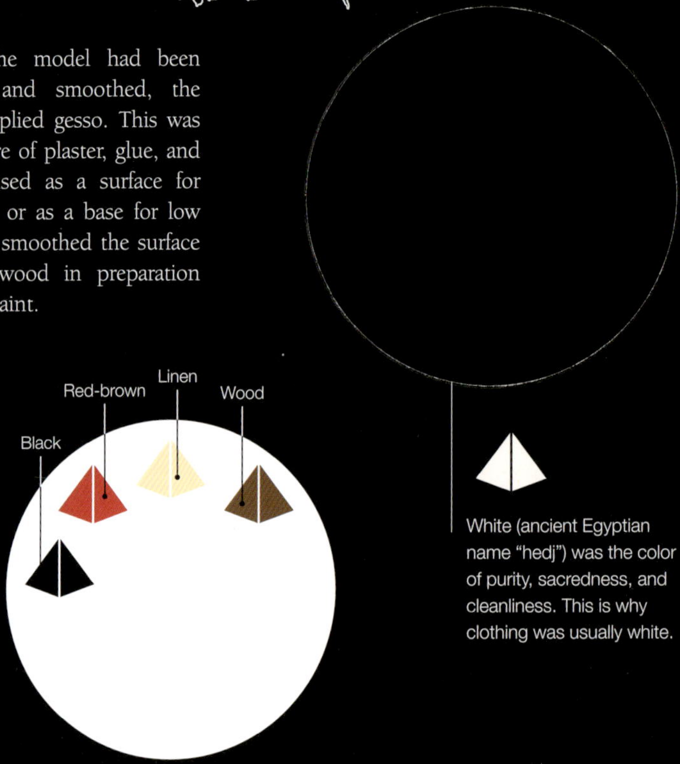

White (ancient Egyptian name "hedj") was the color of purity, sacredness, and cleanliness. This is why clothing was usually white.

Egyptian wood was fairly scarce so the best Egyptian carving was traditionally done in stone, which was also more enduring. Yet for a short time during the Middle Kingdom, woodcarving became more prevalent. Once carved, this model and others like it were painted in flat washes. The pigments were ground on a hard stone with a pestle and mortar and applied by mixing them with plant gum. They were moistened and then applied to the prepared wood. All the figures on the boat are painted a reddish-brown (made with iron oxide and red earth) and wear white kilts of varying lengths. To do this, the artist mixed as much of one color as he needed, painted all the appropriate areas and then moved on to another color. Sometimes this included layering colors over each other to achieve different color effects.

Carpenters and modelmakers usually worked in groups using a sophisticated array of tools: axes cut the trunks into planks; adzes shaped, planed, and shaved; awls and bow drills bored holes; chisels and wooden mallets shaped and cut grooves. Pieces of wood were joined by dowels or tenons and glued together and occasionally metal nails were used. Minor flaws were shaved off with an adze and, in the case of this model, covered with gesso and the artifact painted.

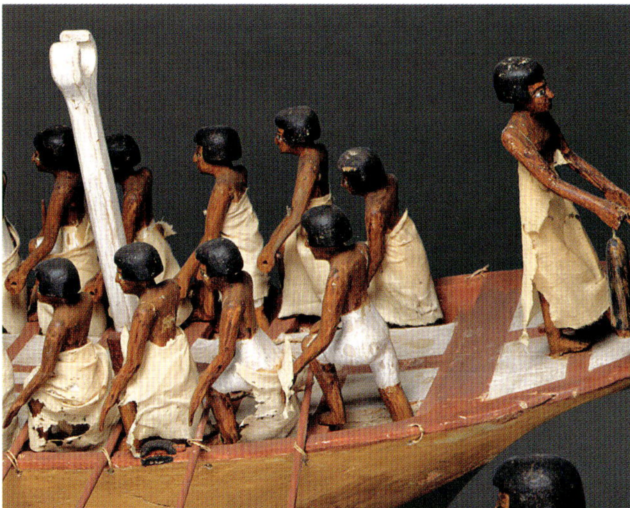

Carved out of several pieces of wood, the pinholes at the figures' shoulders indicate where separately carved arms were attached.

Although painted wooden models showing groups of servants engaged in a variety of activities were often placed in tombs during the Old Kingdom, by the Middle Kingdom additional themes were added including models of workshops showing woodworking, metalworking, and pottery.

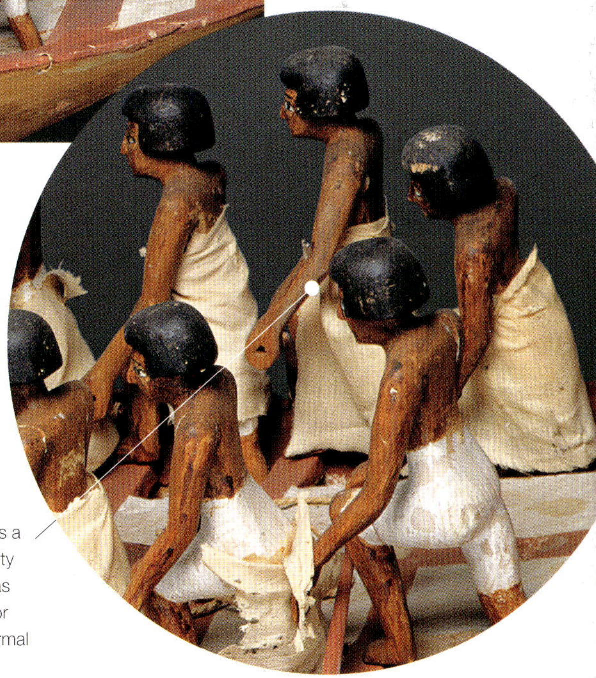

Each figure conveys a feeling of individuality and motion that was seldom achieved, or desired, in more formal Egyptian statuary.

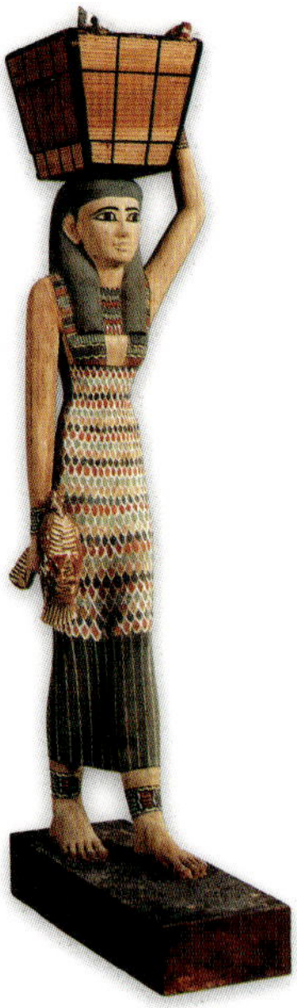

FROM THE TOMB OF MEKETRE, WESTERN THEBES, NOW IN THE METROPOLITAN MUSEUM OF ART, NEW YORK

Statue of an Offering Bearer

Wood, pigment, and gesso,
c.1985 BCE

THIS MODEL IS ONE OF A PAIR OF OFFERING BEARERS from the tomb of the chancellor Meketre in Western Thebes (*see pages 14–19*). When the tomb chamber was opened in 1920, no one had entered it since it had been sealed almost 4,000 years earlier. It was a magnificent find because many wooden models from ancient Egypt have been eaten by termites. The models show the remarkable skill of the artisans of that period. Although limited in their creativity by the

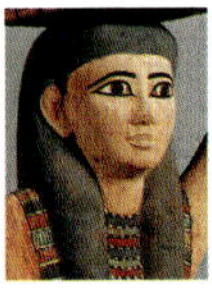

2040–1640 BCE

Period of peace and prosperity in which Egyptian civilization reaches its height

c.2005 BCE

Mentuhotep II builds mortuary temple in Western Thebes worshiping the goddess Hathor

c.2000 BCE

Mentuhotep II's innovative building and artwork anticipates some ideas of the New Kingdom

rules of art, these craftsmen were respected as skillful artisans and were usually considered to be middle class. Models of offering bearers and other servants were placed in tombs in the belief that in the afterlife they would come to life and be available to the tomb owner. Wooden models like this were common in nobles' tombs during the Middle Kingdom and wooden figures appear more relaxed and lifelike than statues and paintings of the period. The opaque paint used on them gives them an almost toylike appearance, but the details in this model indicate the importance that the Egyptians placed on such objects. A deceased person's afterlife depended on the funerary figures being self-explanatory enough to recreate the person's daily life in the next world. This servant holds a live duck by its wings in one hand and balances a basket of food on her head with the other. The other model in the pair carries four jars of drink in her basket so that, between them, the two models ensured that Meketre was provided with both food and drink in the afterlife. Dress in ancient Egypt showed diversity according to class or occupation. Humble people wore a belt or skirt (known as a kilt) tied around the waist—most servants and children did not wear "proper clothes" as this figure does. Her elegant attire indicates that she was linked to the gods and the subtle quality of the carving and painting was intended to inform the gods that Meketre was an important person in his life, so should be treated well in the next.

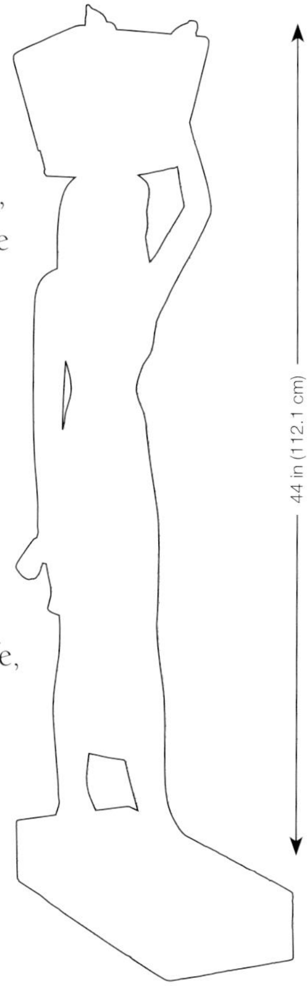

Fact

Most Egyptian art represents women as gentle, passive figures, but since the action of offering is important, female offering-bearers are often shown in full stride—a pose normally reserved for men.

c.2000 BCE

High-ranking officials are buried in tombs with a chapel above the burial shaft

1991–1783 BCE

During the 12th dynasty, the most important god of Thebes is Amun

c.1991 BCE

New grid system for painting and sculpture replaces the Old Kingdom system of guidelines

c.1981–1802 BCE

Egypt reestablishes control of Lower Nubia by building a series of forts

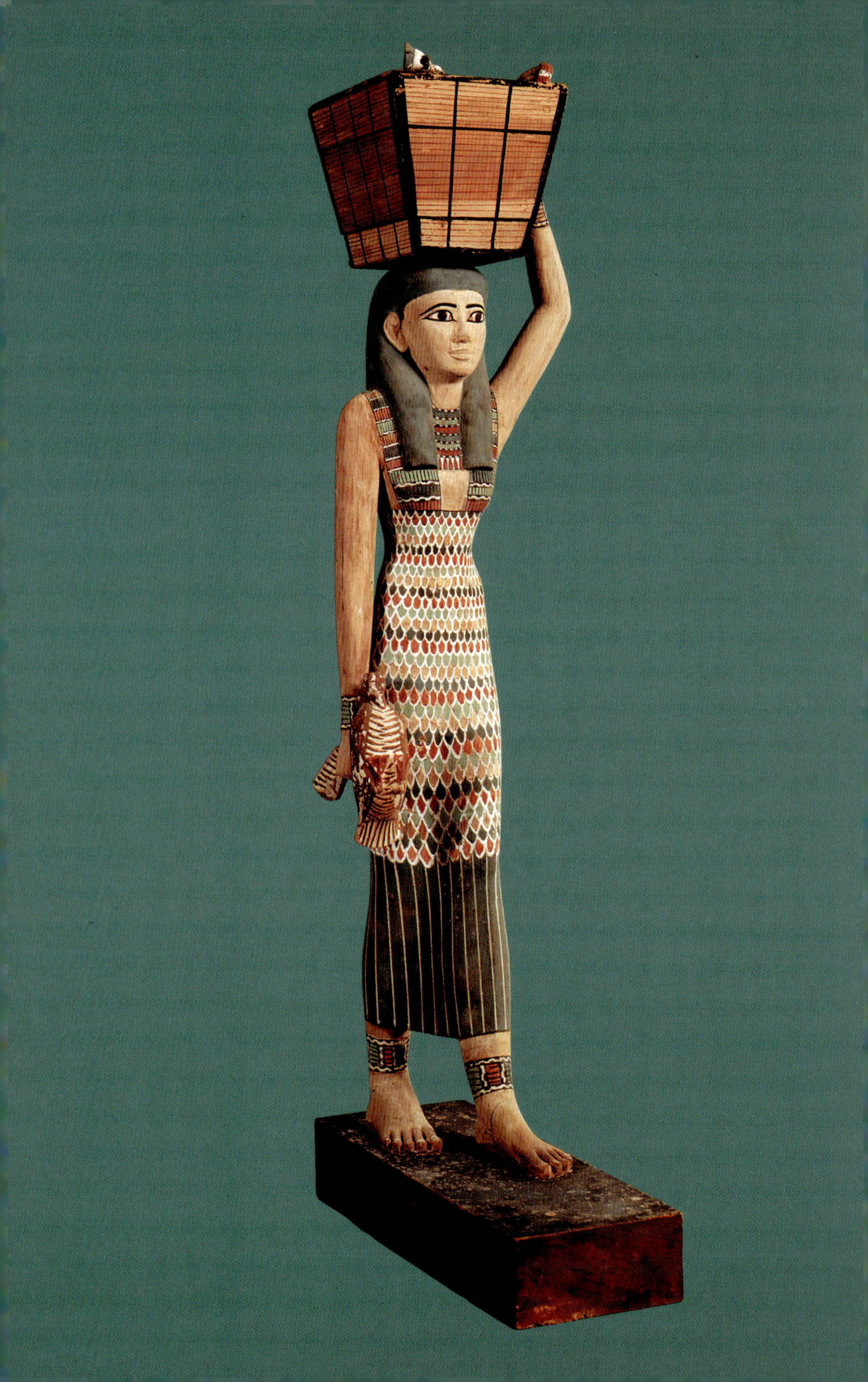

The figure's slender shape indicates what the ancient Egyptians found attractive—it is rare to see an ugly image prepared for the afterlife.

These wooden figures are more dynamic than other Egyptian statues or paintings. This model strides purposefully toward Meketre with her offerings.

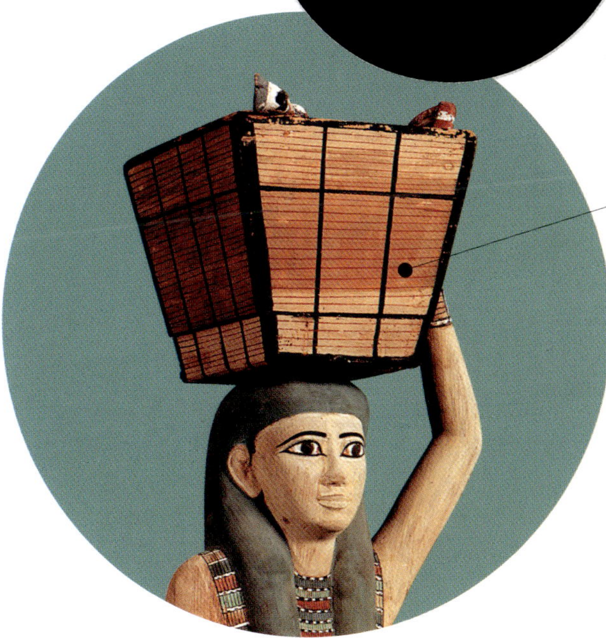

This figure is larger than the other models found in the tomb. Her size, broad collar necklace, bracelets, anklets, and stylish dress indicate her importance and express Middle Kingdom values of paying homage to gods and goddesses. The patterns on her dress represent small feathers and the vertical stripes of the underskirt symbolize long wing feathers. Goddesses are frequently portrayed in similar costumes and here the dress probably refers to Isis or Nephthys, both of whom protected the dead in the afterlife. Killing animals and having a live duck are both symbolic of making order out of a chaotic world and show the honor Meketre's servants had for his spirit—in a similar sentiment to taking flowers to a funeral.

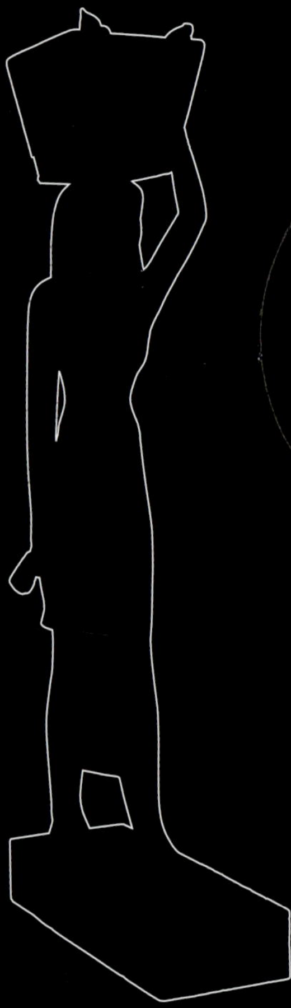

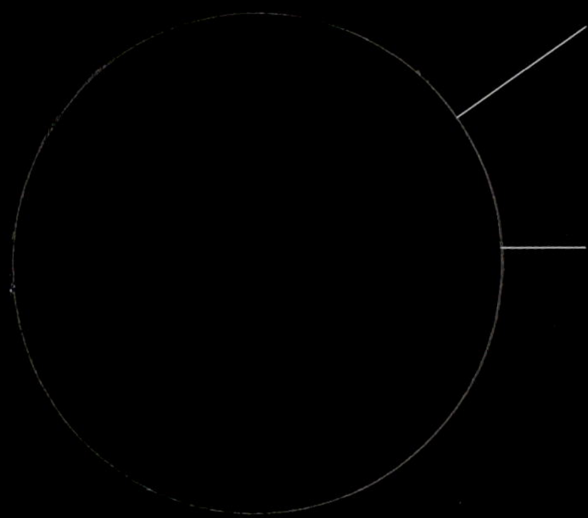

The wig was plastered before painting, but the figure was painted directly onto the wood, in a mixture of pigment and gesso.

Several ancient Egyptian pigments reacted chemically with each other—for example lead white when mixed with orpiment (yellow) resulted in black.

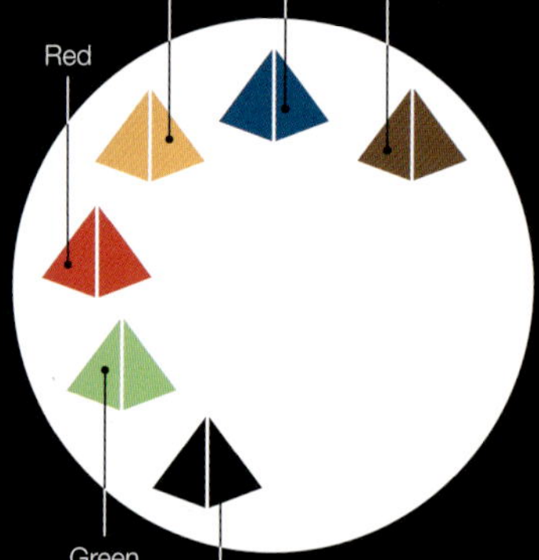

The degree to which ancient Egyptian artists and craftsmen mixed colors varied according to dynasty, but even at its most creative, mixing was not extensive. Each area was completed before moving on to the next because it was considered good practice to keep colors separate.

The whole figure is completely painted, with blue hair (now turned greenish-gray), black eyes and eyebrows, yellow skin, and patterns in red, green, yellow, and blue for the jewelry and dress. There is a remarkable amount of detail on the clothing and jewelry, demonstrating the painstaking process of painting models such as this. Color often symbolized certain things. For instance, the color green ("wadj") represented vegetation and new life. Green pigment could be produced by mixing oxides of copper and iron with silica and calcium. It could also be derived from malachite, a natural copper ore. Red ("djesher") was the color of life and victory and was usually created by using naturally oxidized iron and red ocher.

Since it was scarce, wood was considered sacred in Egypt. Carved from the roughly cylindrical shape of a tree trunk, the squared base and frontal, balanced pose conform to the rectilinear style of stone sculpture. Unlike stone sculpture, however, in wooden figures the space between body and limbs is open, creating a more lifelike appearance.

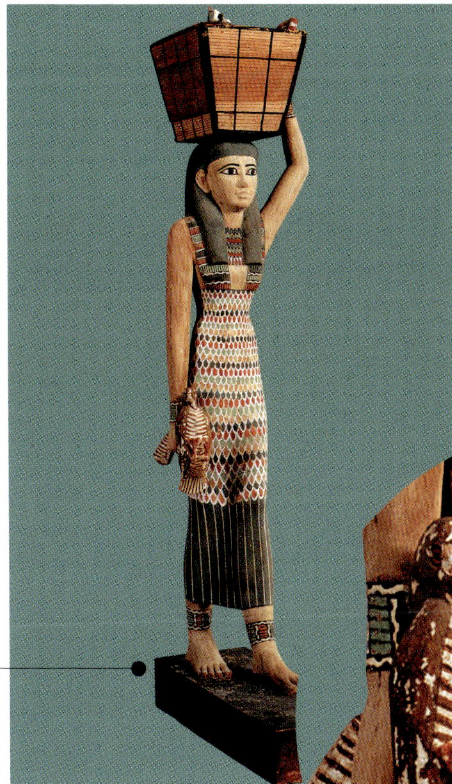

Tenons below the feet attach the figure to the base, which is squared and reflects the angular style of stone sculpture.

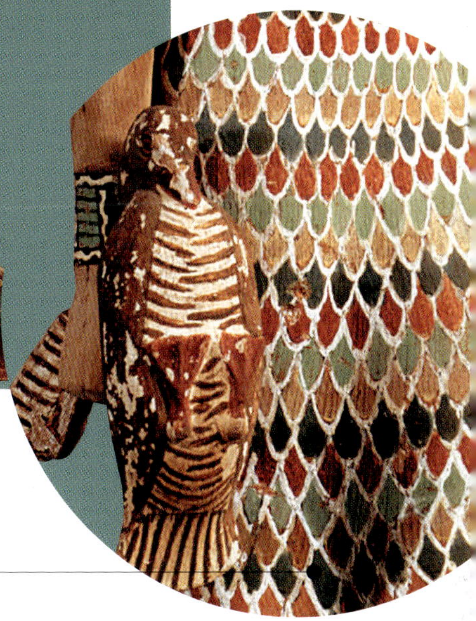

The pattern of the dress was painted to represent feathers—a reference to winged goddesses Isis and Nephthys.

In the Middle Kingdom, artisans' workshops were led by single artists. Here sculptors gathered their apprentices and instructed them. A professional association existed, which was organized with a strict hierarchy. At the top were the highest sculptors, followed by supervisors, ordinary sculptors, and assistants. Similar conventions and restrictions guided artists when carving wood as when carving stone, although the malleability of wood allowed the figure to be more naturalistic than stone statues. This figure is made of coniferous wood, carved from a single cylindrical tree trunk. The head, body, legs, and right foot are carved from one piece, while the arms, base, duck, basket, and front part of the left foot were made separately and then attached to the body with pegs.

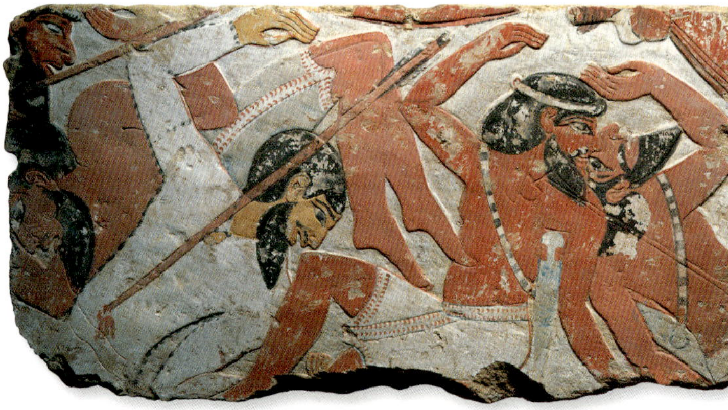

FROM THEBES, PROBABLY DURING REIGN OF THUTMOSE IV, NOW IN THE METROPOLITAN MUSEUM OF ART, NEW YORK

Fragment of a Battle Scene

Painted sandstone,
c.1400–1390 BCE

WHEN THUTMOSE IV CAME TO THE THRONE OF EGYPT in about 1400 BCE, the Sphinx of Giza, made over a thousand years previously for King Khafre (*see pages 8–13*) was buried up to its neck in sand. Legend tells of Thutmose IV falling asleep on the sand near the head of the great Sphinx and dreaming that the spirit of his royal ancestor called upon him to excavate the colossal statue from its sandy incarceration. He awoke and set his men to work, clearing the body of the Sphinx and restoring it to its former glory. Although Thutmose only reigned for about nine years, it was a successful period and a time of wealth and relative peace. As soon as he had excavated the Sphinx, Thutmose

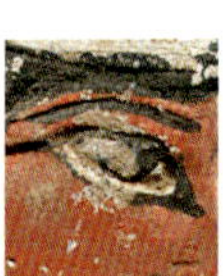

1550–1307 BCE

New Kingdom period of the 18th dynasty, consisting of 14 pharaohs

1473–1458 BCE

Hatshepsut, the 5th pharaoh of the 18th dynasty and one of the most successful queens, rules ancient Egypt

c.1400 BCE

Young, handsome King Thutmose IV inherits the throne of Egypt

began building and added to several temples in Egypt and Nubia (now northern Sudan). Many of his monuments were additions to preexisting temples. This stone block was once part of the façade of a large temple that was already standing in the Asasif region of Thebes.

It might seem a dichotomy that a large battle scene was created on the outside of a temple, but it symbolized the king triumphing over the forces of chaos and disorder. To the Egyptians, this was an important part of their beliefs—chaos had to be controlled and this helped to avert evil from the sanctuary of the temple. The relief shows part of a large battle portraying Thutmose riding in a chariot over wounded, dying, and defeated enemies. The pointed beards and moustaches of the fallen men identify them as being from western Asia, possibly from the area of modern Syria. Since the time of the previous pharaoh, Thutmose III, Egypt had become embroiled in a struggle for control of Syria and Palestine, so although there were no major battles during Thutmose IV's reign, there were certainly some minor conflicts. The relief shows defeated enemies and was an appropriate motif for the outside of a temple wall because it shows the king's conquest over evil forces, and his ability to maintain cosmic order, or *maat*. Treasure from the defeated enemy would be distributed among the Egyptian soldiers after some successful battles. Acts of courage were rewarded with grants of land, tomb sites, or elaborate gifts such as gold necklaces or military medals.

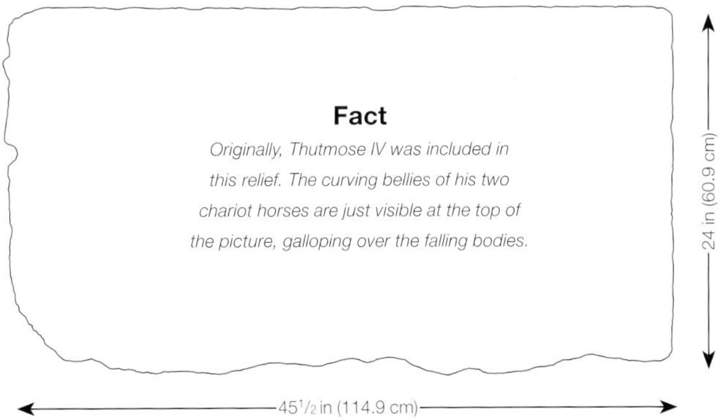

Fact

Originally, Thutmose IV was included in this relief. The curving bellies of his two chariot horses are just visible at the top of the picture, galloping over the falling bodies.

1400 BCE

Thebes, the capital of Egypt, becomes the largest city in the world

c.1400 BCE

Possible date for Biblical account of the Ten Commandments being delivered to Moses

c.1393 BCE

The "dream stela" is carved on the Sphinx, relating Thutmose IV's excavation of the Sphinx

c.1390 BCE

Thutmose IV dies young and is buried in a tomb in the Valley of the Kings

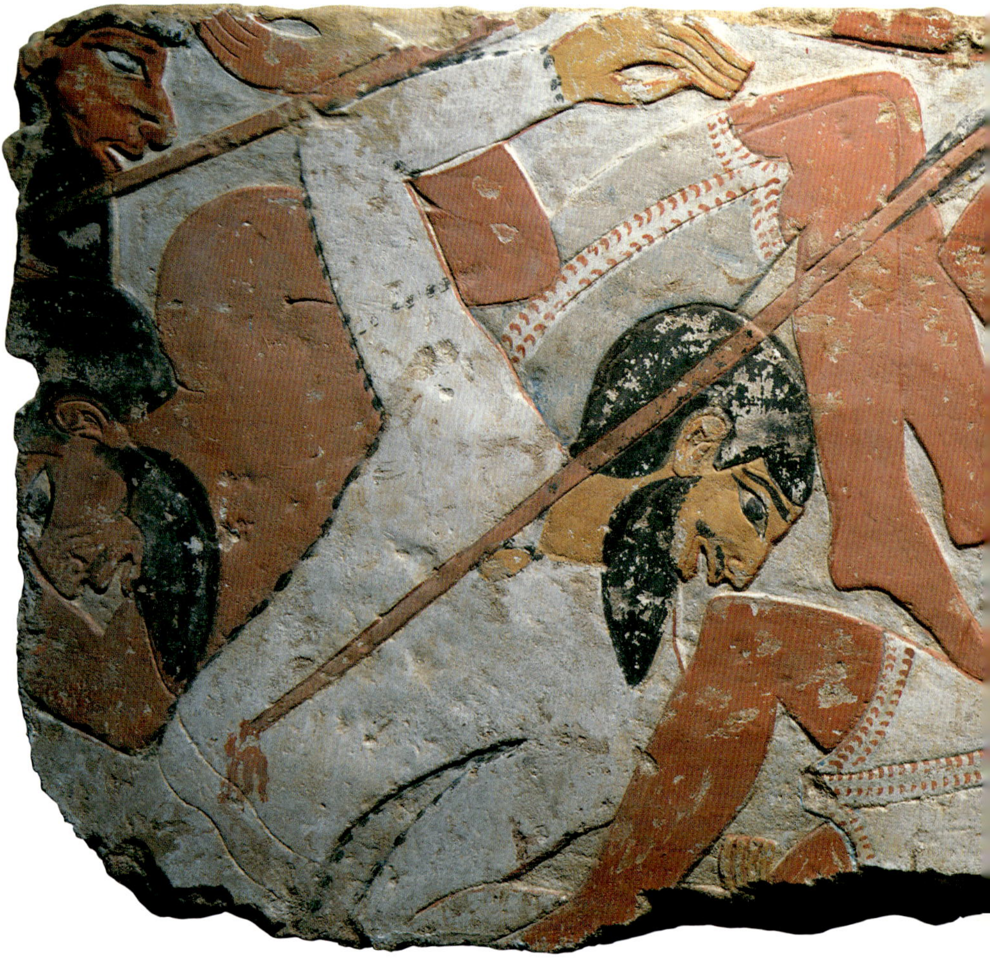

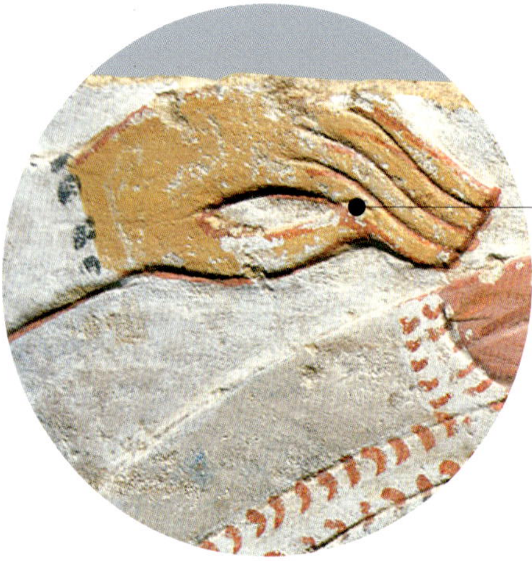

Hands are always depicted in the same way, no matter if they are left or right—and always with long, slim fingers and fingernails.

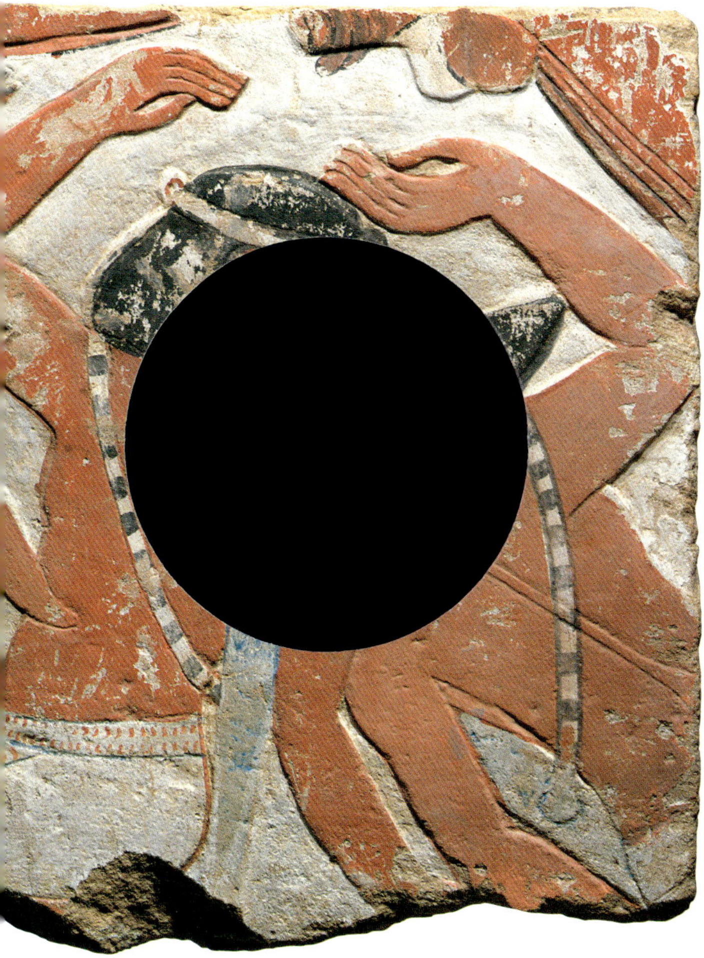

For several thousand years, the Egyptians were consistent in their representations, always showing things in their most recognized form. For example, they always showed the human body in its most instructive way, not because they thought they looked like that. Heads are most clearly seen in profile, but eyes are more familiar from the front. The top half of the body, shoulders, and chest are best seen from the front because that shows how arms are attached to the shoulders, but arms and legs in movement are more clearly seen from the side. The Egyptians also represented people of other nationalities in a stereotypical way, regardless of what they might actually have looked like. So Syrians in Egyptian art are always shown as having long, pointed beards and often long, round-tipped noses. In this shallow relief, these rules have been adhered to, but the artists have also tried to create energy and depth. Even though it was originally drawn on a grid, the diagonal angles create a sense of action. The artists have not tried to model the figures and give them a solid appearance; they are still essentially diagrams to give information, but their flailing limbs and falling weapons represent the skirmish quite vividly.

Artists applied a layer of gesso to the limestone before applying the paint, made using ground mineral pigments combined with plant gum or glue made from animals. They applied the paint in broad strokes using thick brushes, one color at a time, with no shading or effects of light.

By this time, Egyptian artists were using white lead more frequently than chalk for white paint because it was more opaque and longer lasting.

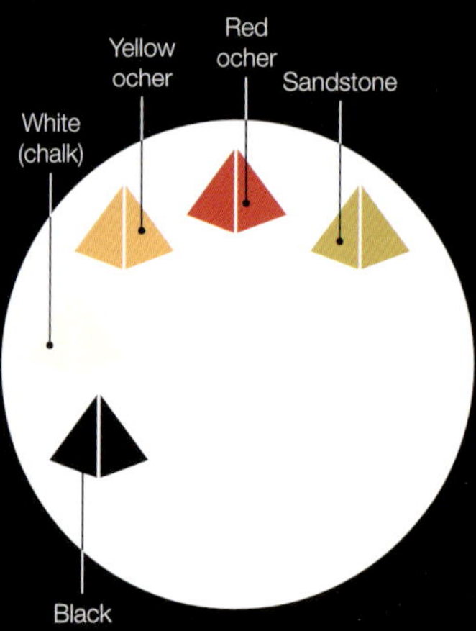

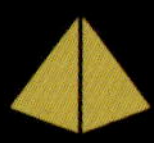

The colors have remained remarkably fresh for a limestone relief because this block was reused in building the foundations of a later temple. Skin was painted mainly with red earth or iron oxide.

Before painting a relief, assistant or apprentice artists drew squared grids on the surface of the limestone to help them obtain the correct proportions of the scene. Next, a master draftsman sketched the image, firstly in red and then in black. Other artists chipped away around the main figures to create the shallow relief that would throw cast shadows, helping the images to stand out in the sunlight. Originally, sunken relief was designed to decorate exterior walls, when figures were cut back to a slightly lower level than the background, but some pharaohs preferred the effects of raised reliefs. The artists adhered to the conventions of depicting the human body with the shoulders and eyes in front view and the arms, legs, and heads in profile.

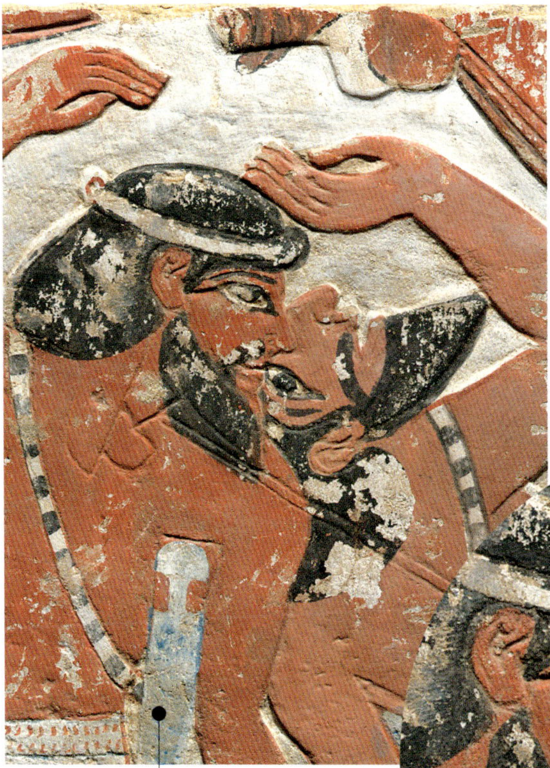

Even though this seems more expressive than traditional Egyptian art, it still conformed to conventions, including a harmonious balance of shapes, proportion, and lines. It was not intended to lead anyone to the next life, but it was Egyptian propaganda—for the people and the gods.

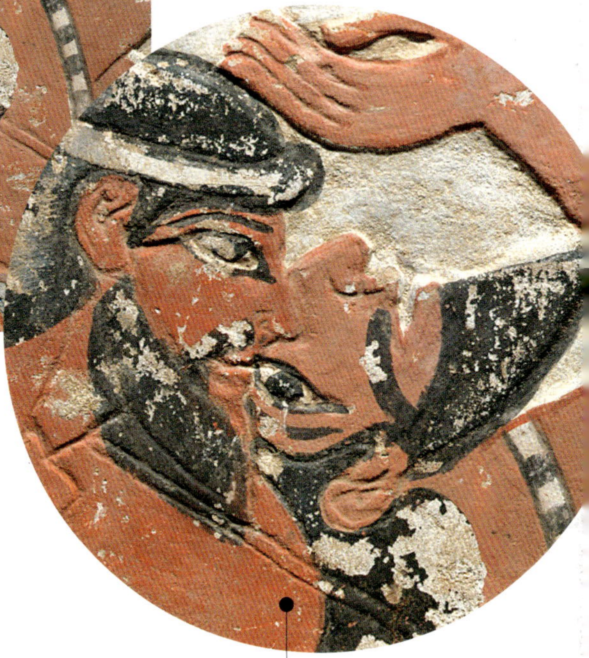

The men's sashes and other details were picked out with a thin brush.

Although this relief is more dynamic than many other images of the time, the method of representing everything remained essentially the same. As the men tumble beneath the horses' hooves, they overlap, but there is no impression of real depth. This is due partly to the lack of foreshortening and modeling and partly because the paint was applied in flat colors. The relief is very shallow—the background was cut away scarcely a quarter of an inch. Everything interacts, expressing the confusion, terror, and fear of being trapped in hand-to-hand combat. Equally effective are the diagonal lines formed by arms, legs, torsos, and arrows and the repetitions of heads, curved hands, beards, and white clothes. The hands are particularly expressive and different from traditional Egyptian art.

Color was applied with coarse brushes made from bundles of palm fibers, or pieces of fibrous wood chewed or beaten at one end.

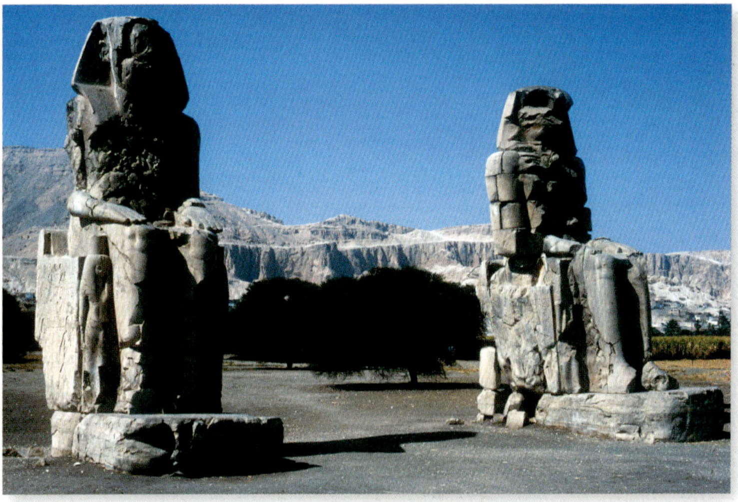

WEST BANK OF THE NILE, THEBES, MODERN LUXOR

The Colossi of Amenhotep III

Quartzite sandstone,
c.1375 BCE

DURING THE 18TH DYNASTY, temples dedicated to various gods became larger and more important than before. As always, kings were responsible for their construction and 18th-dynasty pharaohs in particular built widely throughout the major centers of Upper and Lower Egypt and Nubia. Old and Middle Kingdom temples built of mud brick were replaced by great complexes of limestone or sandstone that were entered through massive gateways with tall towers on either side. King Amenhotep III built the largest and most opulent funerary complex that had ever been constructed at Thebes, where he would have been worshiped as a god both before and after his death. All that remains of

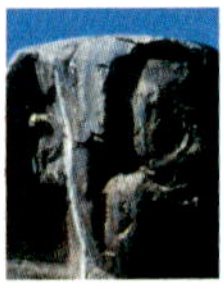

c.2700–1450 BCE

Time of the Minoan civilization, a Bronze Age civilization that arose on Crete

c.1600–1100 BCE

Mycenaean civilization flourishes on mainland Greece—a sophisticated period of art, literature, and myth

c.1450 BCE

Mycenaean artists adopt many Minoan styles but Mycenaean art is grander and less spontaneous

the complex now are the two imposing statues that guarded the outer gates. Their function was to inspire awe at the king's power and to celebrate Egyptian achievements. Their size and location made them visible from a distance, even to people who were barred from entering the temple grounds. Even now, despite being badly damaged by nature and ancient tourists, the two colossal statues still sit gazing eastward toward the Nile and the rising sun. Although both represent Amenhotep III, the northern statue (on the right side of the image on page 32) is of the pharaoh with his mother, Mutemwia, and the southern statue is of him with his wife Tiy and one of their daughters. Together these women represented Hathor, the goddess of the sky. Hathor was both mother and consort to the sun god, so she represented love and motherhood. The ancient Greeks thought that the statues represented King Memnon, a hero of the Trojan War who was ultimately killed by Achilles, and they called the entire temple complex the Memnonium after him.

After an earthquake in 27 BCE, damage to the statues caused a light moaning sound to be emitted from the right-hand statue each morning, probably due to rising temperatures and humidity. Anyone who heard the "singing" was thought to be about to experience good luck, so a constant stream of visitors, including Hadrian and his empress Sabina, visited the statues for centuries. Unfortunately, in 199 CE, the Roman Emperor Septimius Severus attempted to repair the statues but unintentionally silenced them forever.

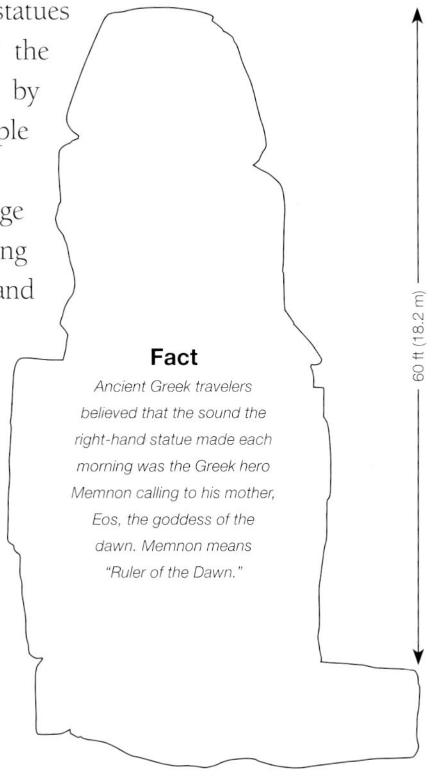

Fact

Ancient Greek travelers believed that the sound the right-hand statue made each morning was the Greek hero Memnon calling to his mother, Eos, the goddess of the dawn. Memnon means "Ruler of the Dawn."

1391–1353 BCE

Amenhotep III rules over a peaceful country and increases monument building

c.1390–1352 BCE

Egyptian water clocks now indicate the passage of hours of the night by regulated water flow

c.1375 BCE

Colossi of Amenhotep constructed at the site of Amenhotep's great mortuary temple

1350 BCE

Yin dynasty begins in China, becoming the golden age of the Shang dynasty

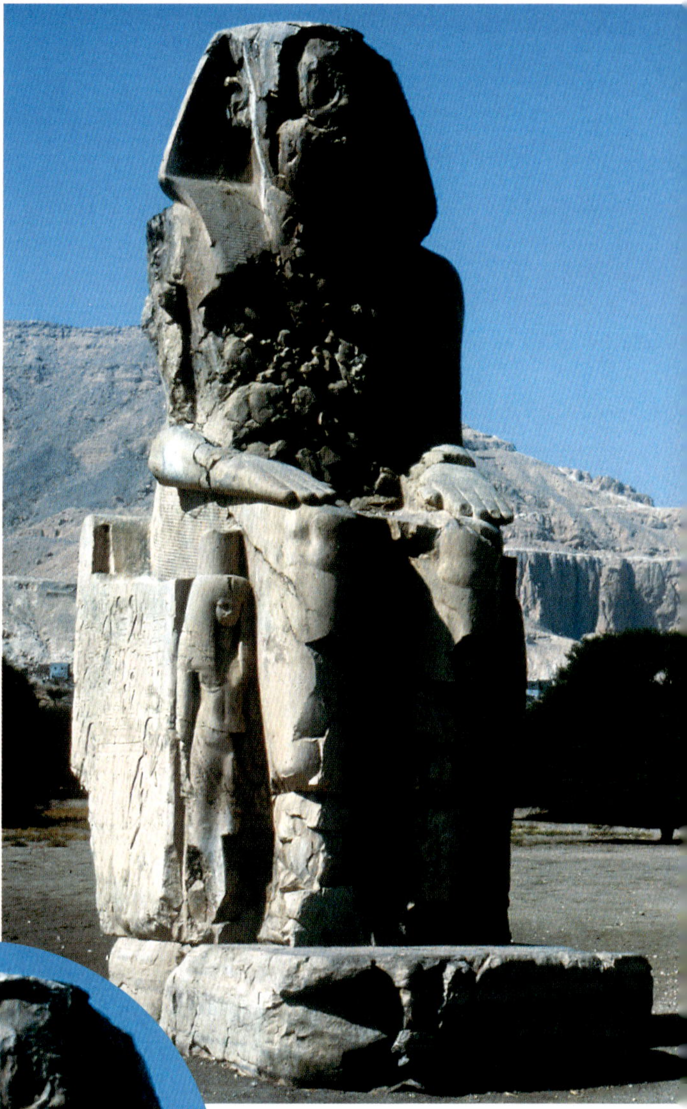

Although the faces have eroded, on this statue you can still see the *nemes* (striped headdress worn by pharaohs) and remains of the false beard.

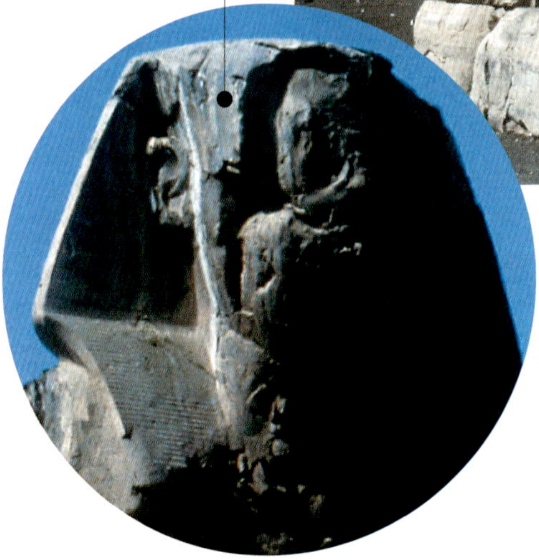

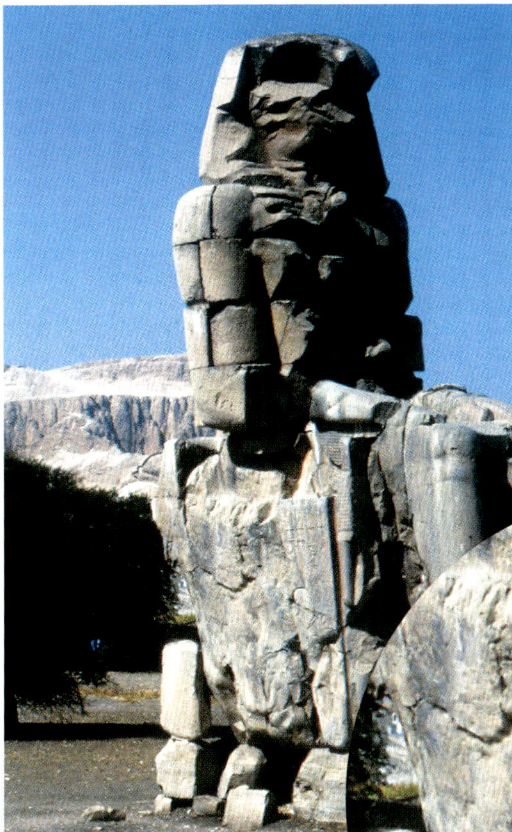

Assistants marked grids on each side of the stone blocks, using string dipped in paint at vertical and horizontal intervals. The figures were then drawn directly onto the grids by the outline draftsmen, who scaled up the work from designs on papyrus. Stonemasons then chipped away around the drawing.

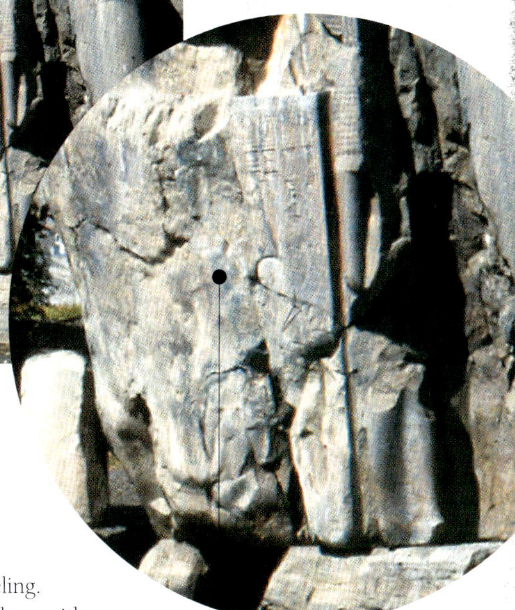

On the sides of the statue, hieroglyphs and other symbols tell of the pharoah and of Egypt's unity.

The size of sculpture reflected the social order, so these statues were clearly of a pharaoh or god. Since artists did not free the sculpted form from the block of stone, they had to be solidly designed and adhered to strict rules. There were only three options for statue figures: standing, sitting, or kneeling. Extracting materials from hard-stone quarries was done with either metal tools or with tools made from harder stone. For these colossi, quartzite was removed from quarries over 400 miles away by building steps into vertical walled trenches, then breaking off the quartzite blocks with huge diorite chisels. Once in position, using pulleys and levers, the blocks of stone were assembled at the right heights and widths for carving.

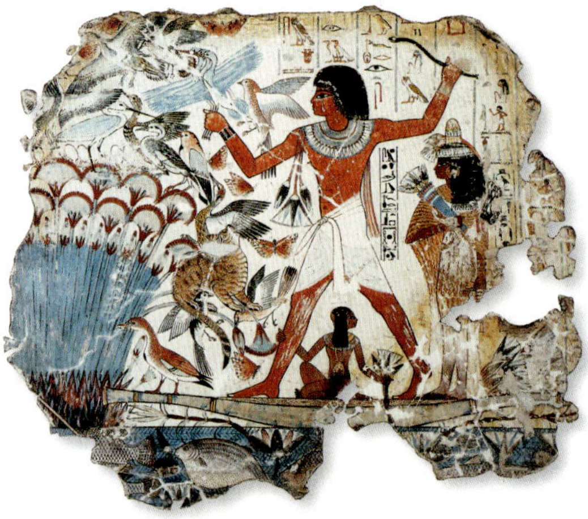

FROM THE TOMB OF NEBAMUN, THEBES, NOW IN THE BRITISH MUSEUM, LONDON

Fowling in the Marshes

Fresco secco,
c.1356 BCE

THIS IS ONE OF SEVERAL WALL PAINTINGS found in the tomb of the powerful statesman Nebamun. Ancient Egyptian society consisted of the nobility, who owned much of the land; the middle class, consisting of merchants, artists, and civil servants; and serfs. Nebamun was part of the nobility. When he died in about 1356 BCE his tomb was richly decorated to ensure a smooth transition to the afterlife. The paintings are typical of the New Kingdom—less rigid than those of earlier periods, but still illustrating the afterlife for the deceased. The New Kingdom was a time of great artistic flowering, when more wall paintings and sculptures were produced and new techniques

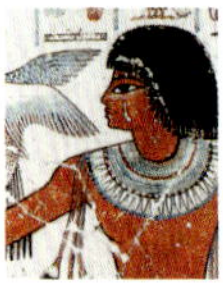

1550 BCE

The 18th Dynasty begins, and Egypt experiences a new period of artistic freedom

1540 BCE

Egyptian gods begin to be grouped together in paintings, emphasizing the family unit

1540 BCE

Instead of pyramids, tombs for royalty and nobility were made in deserted valleys by Thebes

tried out. Adjacent paintings in this tomb included a banquet and a scribe conducting a goose census on Nebamun's estate. It is an idealized image, created to calm the chaos of this world into order and reason in the next. The fragile painting is remarkably well preserved and the artist's skill is apparent in the dynamic design and richness of detail. Although Nebamun is shown hunting, he might never have hunted during his life. Symbolism was important for establishing a sense of order, and hunting animals symbolized the removal of disorder.

The large fish is a tilapia, which, when danger threatens, takes its young into its mouth to protect them, releasing them when danger has passed. It may imply that Nebamun will be protected as he begins a new life in the next world. Alternatively, it could be viewed as a symbol of self-regeneration. Although Nebamun wears just a linen kilt and elaborate collar, his wife Hatshepsut is dressed for a banquet. Their daughter wears her hair in a side-lock, earrings, and a decorative collar. The family would not have gone hunting together but the picture serves to keep them together in the afterlife. Nebamun is about to throw a snake-headed stick at a flock of birds and holds three herons in his other hand. The hieroglyphs underneath his raised arm explain that he is "taking recreation and seeing what is good in the place of eternity." Cats were often used as hunting companions and his extraordinarily realistic cat has caught three birds in its mouth and paws.

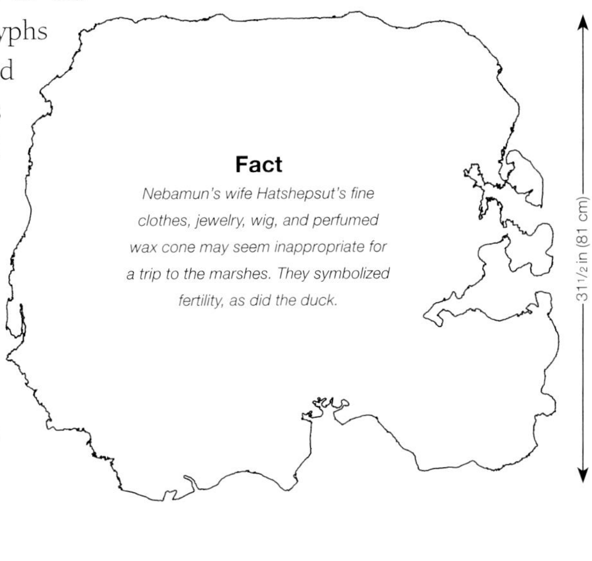

Fact

Nebamun's wife Hatshepsut's fine clothes, jewelry, wig, and perfumed wax cone may seem inappropriate for a trip to the marshes. They symbolized fertility, as did the duck.

c.1380 BCE	1356 BCE	1353 BCE	1341 BCE
Egyptian artists begin drawing figures in slightly more natural poses	The artists who decorate Nebamun's tomb aim for more realism than hitherto	Amenophis IV takes the throne, calls himself Akhenaten and begins worshiping a single god, Aten	Tutankhamen is born and becomes pharaoh in 1333 BCE

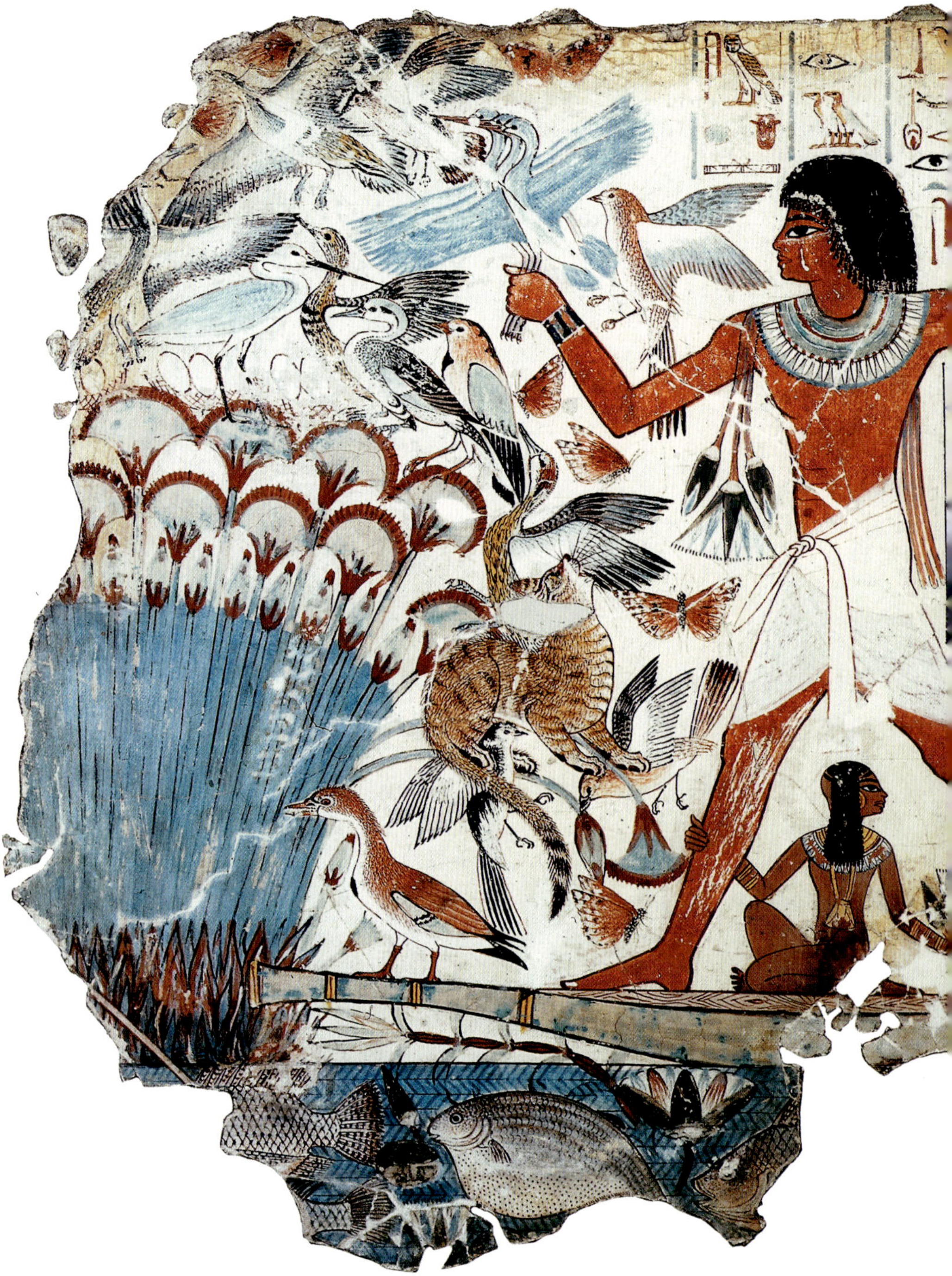

sitions of each figure were carefully planned for
alance and convention. Nebamun is the largest and
nportant. Hatshepsut standing behind him is next
as was the rule for men and women in art, and their
er, of less importance than either adult, is shown
and even smaller than her parents. Overlapping
and the tiny sliver of the inside of the boat suggest
which was also unusual for Egyptian artists. Even
it was not meant to be seen, the artists' skills are
the composition and in the ways in which paint
en applied. What's more, some of the animals,
ally the cat, are shown with more realism and
nism than in earlier works and although figures
re still assembled with faces, arms, and legs in
profile and eyes and chests viewed from the front,
Nebamun is shown actively striding forward.

Placed behind Nebamun in the space between his raised arm and torso, his wife Hatshepsut wears a traditional perfumed waxed cone intended to melt onto her wig.

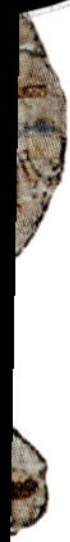

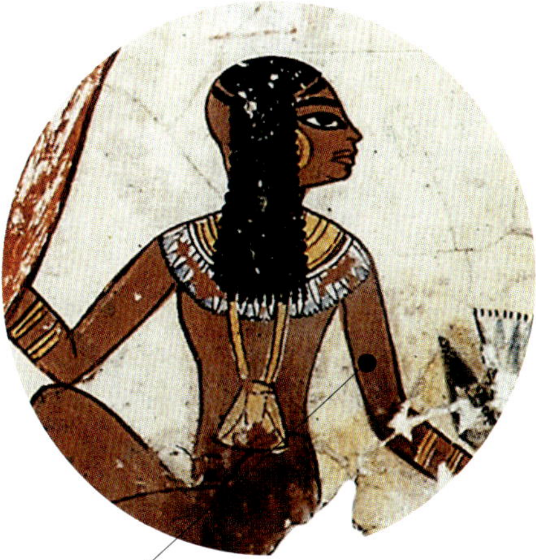

It was common for daughters to be shown in artworks rather than sons because they symbolized fertility.

This mural and others from the same tomb were pair of mud and gypsum using the few pigments that wer to artists of the time and mixed with egg to make ten importance of Egyptian art was reflected in the use o pigments. Earlier in the New Kingdom, gray backgrou been favored but, by the time of Nebamun's death, w backgrounds were preferred. White paint was made f limestone. Reddish skin, tips of the papyrus, and son feathers came from naturally oxidized iron and red oc created from carbon compounds such as soot, groun burned animal bones, and gray-blue was made by mi copper oxides with chalk.

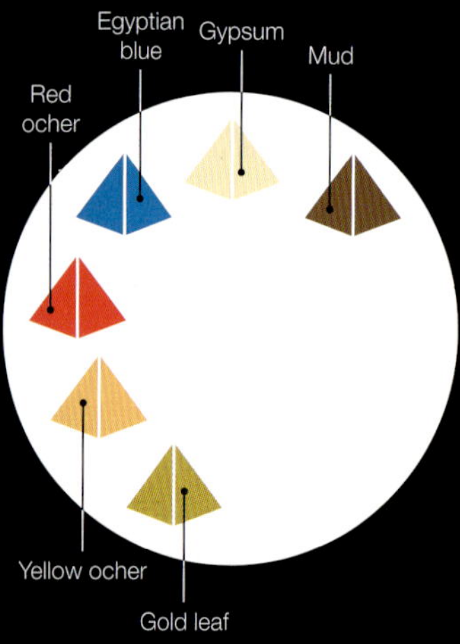

Egyptian blue, the oldest synthetic pigment, was used considerably in the painting. A blend of chalk or limestone, copper oxide, and sand, it had to be fired at extremely high temperatures. The resulting brittle blue material was then ground into a powder.

Paint was applied to the wall in flat tones, although a textural effect has been created on the cat's fur, birds' feathers, and fish scales. Animal textures are one of the few areas where Egyptian artists tried creating illusions of reality.

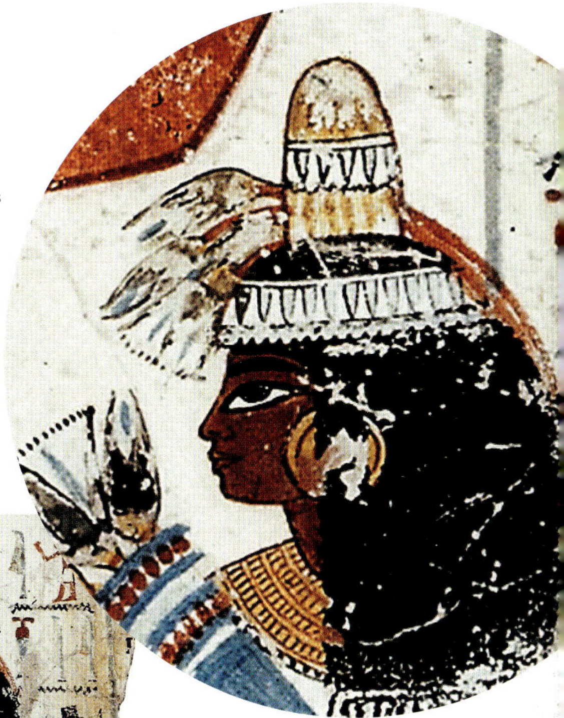

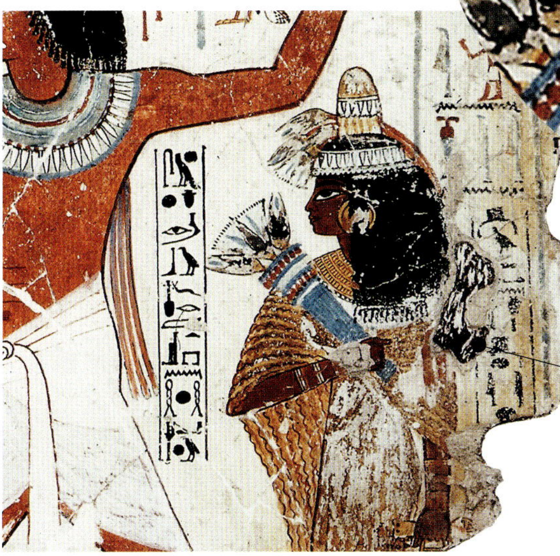

The technique used here is called *fresco secco*—painting with water-soluble colors on dry white plaster. Pigments adhered to the dry surface, so colors remained bright and the painting could be done carefully over time.

Creating tones and overlapping elements in the image were new ways of suggesting three dimensions.

Since the colors were opaque, alterations could be made by overpainting. Unusually, this has a fairly free painterly style, looser than murals of earlier times. Although this is a well-organized design, the painting is action-packed. Momentarily, every creature represented seems to have broken free of established constraints. However, even though this painting was more naturalistic than older tomb paintings, artists adhered to a strict plan. They smoothed the walls then, using string soaked with paint, they marked on a precise grid. Next, trainee artists drew the outlines of the picture, following a sketch on papyrus drawn by a professional artist. Finally, the picture was painted in both the traditional way and using some originality.

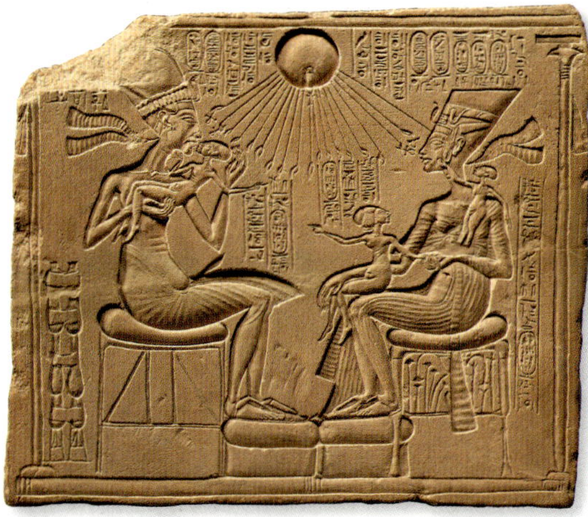

FROM AMARNA, NOW IN THE ALTES MUSEUM, BERLIN

Akhenaten and his Family

Limestone relief,
1353–1336 BCE

THIS LIMESTONE RELIEF WAS PROBABLY PART OF A FAMILY ALTAR in the residence of King Akhenaten who ruled during the 18th dynasty. He ascended to the throne as Amenhotep IV, succeeding his father Amenhotep III. Soon after becoming pharaoh, he discarded his royal name, turned away from the established religion and its priesthood and began the cult of the sun disk—the Aten. His reign lasted for about 17 years, but it is remembered for the radical changes he made to the accepted beliefs. Prior to his reign, up to 2,000 gods were worshiped in Egypt, but Akhenaten created the world's first monotheistic religion in worshiping only Aten, the source of life and light. The impact of suspending all other gods was huge and the priests of Thebes considered the

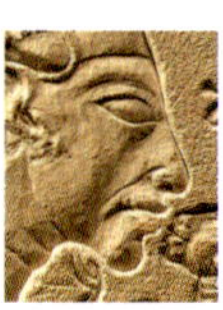

1352–1336 BCE

Reign of Akhenaten, later known as Egypt's "heretic king"

1348 BCE

Work starts on four temples dedicated to the god Aten at Thebes

1346 BCE

Work commences on new city at Akhetaten (modern Amarna) in honor of Aten cult an act of heresy, so Akhenaten built a new court on the east bank of the Nile at Akhetaten (modern Amarna). There he and his wife Nefertiti built a massive city filled with new architecture and art. Since the king's power was absolute, people followed him in their thousands whether they agreed with the new religion or not and, at its height, Akhetaten el-Amarna was inhabited by about 20,000 people. The prominence given to Aten and the inconsequence of other gods helped to initiate the development of more naturalistic art styles and changes in architecture, although some artistic changes can be traced back to Amenhotep III. For the first time in Egypt's history, the artists tried to create images that focused on life, not death.

Stelae—stone slabs decorated with paintings, reliefs, or texts to commemorate an event—were produced as both religious and decorative objects. This stela was probably placed in a small shrine in a private household. It is markedly different from earlier Egyptian art in the relaxed poses, symbols, and style in which it was made. But within 20 years of the new capital being built, it was abandoned. Later pharaohs attempted to erase all memories of Akhenaten and his religion. Much of the distinctive art of the period was destroyed and the buildings dismantled to be reused.

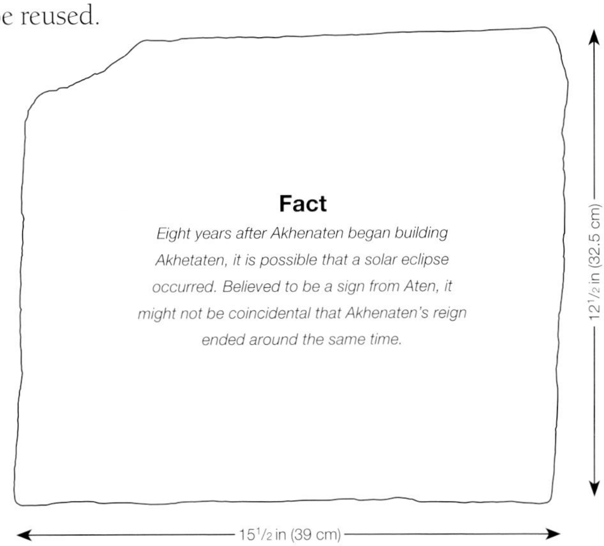

Fact

Eight years after Akhenaten began building Akhetaten, it is possible that a solar eclipse occurred. Believed to be a sign from Aten, it might not be coincidental that Akhenaten's reign ended around the same time.

c.1345 BCE

Several limestone stelae of Akhenaten and his family are carved

1344 BCE

Most of Akhetaten (modern Amarna) is completed and Amenhotep IV changes his name to Akhenaten

1342 BCE

Seat of government is transferred to Akhetaten.

1338 BCE

A solar eclipse may have occurred over Amarna on May 14th in the 15th year of Akhenaten's reign

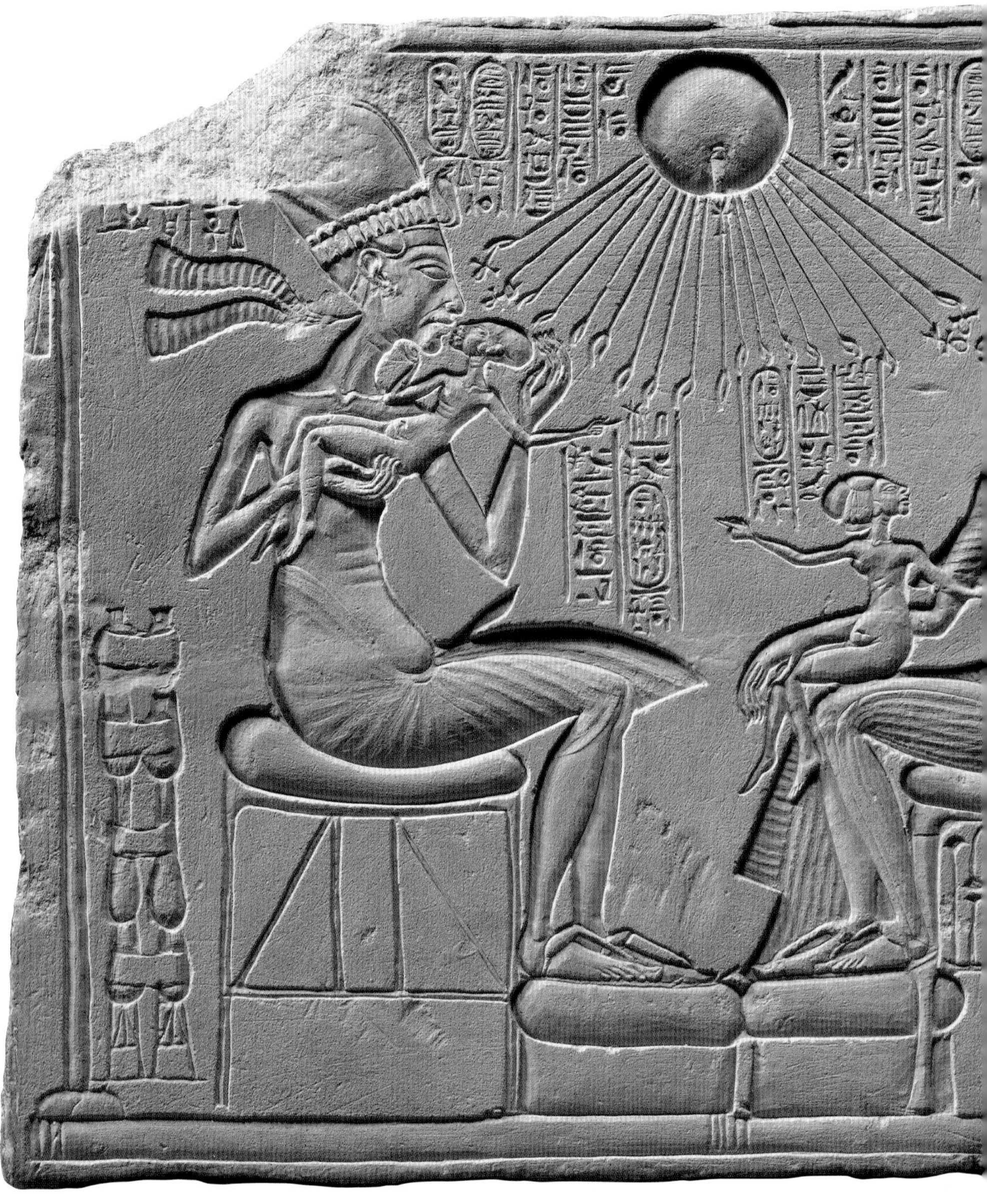

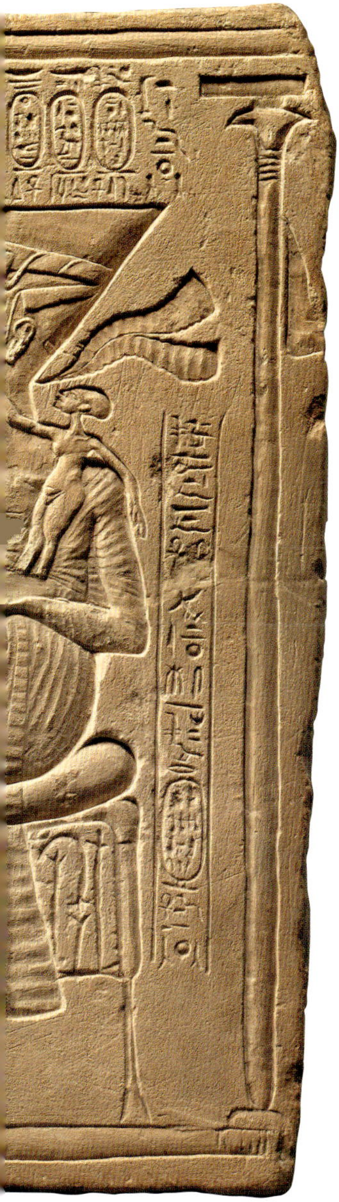

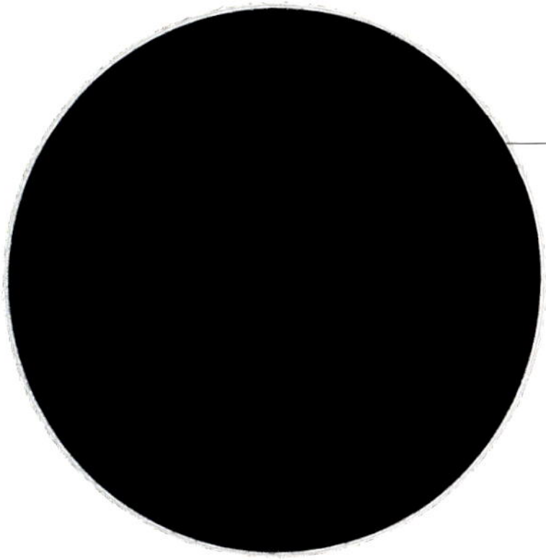

In this intimate scene of royal family life, Ankhesenpaaten, the smallest daughter, plays with her mother's earring in an exceptionally human moment.

Composed as a view through a square window, this new kind of spontaneous representation posed unfamiliar problems to sculptors.

In a relaxed and intimate moment, Akhenaten and his family are portrayed facing each other, on informal stools. Akhenaten's figure is given the traditional primary right-facing orientation and Nefertiti the secondary left-facing one. The children symbolize the continuous process of creation. Akhenaten raises his eldest daughter Meritaten in his arms for a kiss as she points to her mother. Two of the royal couple's younger daughters sit on Nefertiti's lap opposite. Mekeaten gazes lovingly at her mother and Ankhesenpaaten sits on the Queen's shoulder. Akhenaten is depicted wearing the blue crown—frequently described as the war crown—and a pleated kilt, while Nefertiti is shown wearing her characteristic high crown and a traditional long robe that is held in place with a belt. At the top of the composition, the sun god, Aten, represented by a raised circle, extends his life-giving rays to the royal family.

Limestone was available locally at Amarna—only especially good limestone needed to be brought from Memphis in the north.

This relief provides an insight to both Akhenaten's theological position of power and his closeness to the populace with its image of close family life.

Inscriptions tell us that the king himself instructed artists in the new style. Yet he did not change everything. Although this relief uses the concept of a snapshot of life, it is still not lifelike. According to tradition even older children had to be shown smaller than their parents so even though Meritaten is an adolescent, she is portrayed as small as a baby. It was not the real height that mattered, but the "scale of importance." Unusually, therefore, Nefertiti is almost the same size as her husband, when traditional Egyptian art depicted wives—even queens—as smaller than their husbands. Nevertheless in other ways, Egyptian rules of art had been flouted and this distinguished the creative output in what has become known as the Amarna period.

While size conventions adhered, actions, gestures, and body shapes changed. The backs of the princesses' heads protrude oddly. The figures have thin arms and long necks and Akhenaten has a paunch. In other works he is shown with femininely curved hips.

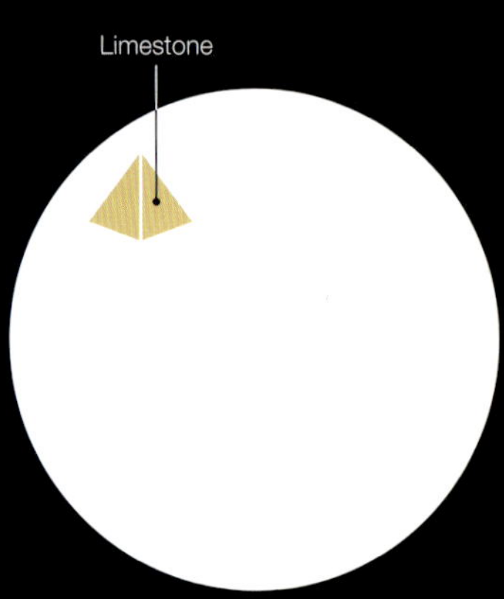

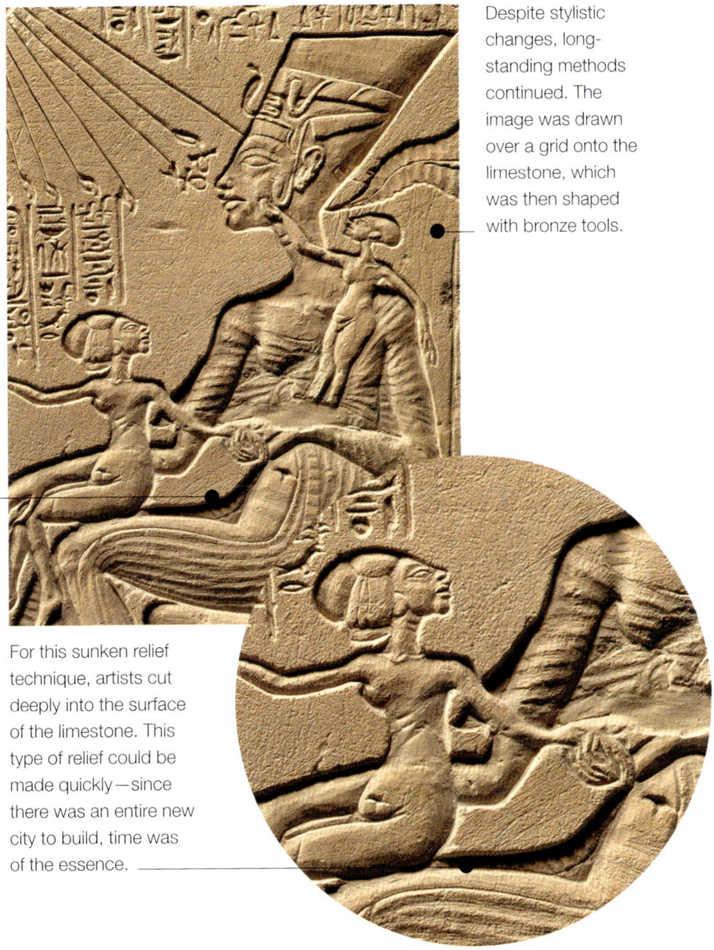

Despite stylistic changes, long-standing methods continued. The image was drawn over a grid onto the limestone, which was then shaped with bronze tools.

Nefertiti, like her husband, was depicted with a long face, forehead, and chin, full lips, and elongated eyes and neck. It may have been a close likeness or a stylistic method the king preferred.

For this sunken relief technique, artists cut deeply into the surface of the limestone. This type of relief could be made quickly—since there was an entire new city to build, time was of the essence.

The sunrays reaching down had never been seen before in Egyptian art. Some of the rays are handing the royal couple the ankh, the symbol of life. These rays were put only on images that included the pharaoh because it was accepted that the pharaoh was the only mortal able to communicate with the gods. The image summarized Akhenaten's ideology—that the sun god wanted direct contact only with his son Akhenaten. Akhenaten's direct contact with Aten was also demonstrated by the diminished power of the priests at the time. The royal family is not represented here as perfect humans in an ideal life after death, but shown alive in this world, displaying human emotions.

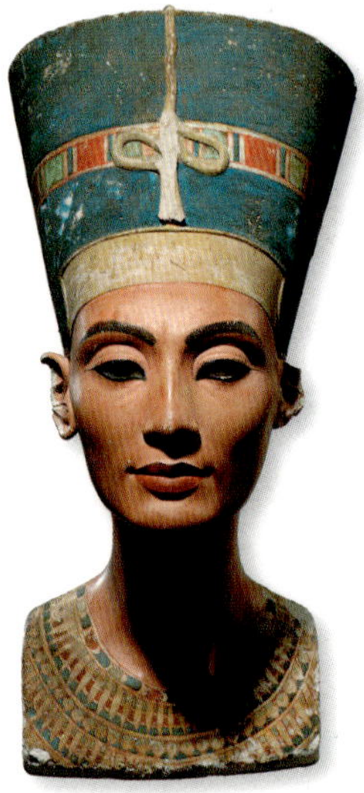

FROM THE WORKSHOP OF SCULPTOR TUTHMOSIS IN AMARNA,
NOW IN THE ALTES MUSEUM, BERLIN

Crowned Head of Queen Nefertiti

Painted limestone,
c.1340 BCE

NEFERTITI, THE WIFE OF THE REBEL KING AKHENATEN and mother-in-law of Tutankhamen during the 18th dynasty, is probably one of the best-known queens of ancient Egypt. Unusually, her face appears in more artwork than that of her husband and she is considered one of the most beautiful women of the ancient world. At the age of 21, the Egyptian pharaoh Amenhotep IV (later Akhenaten), renounced his ties to the religion of his time by moving the capital of Egypt from Thebes to a new site, Amarna. Amenhotep named

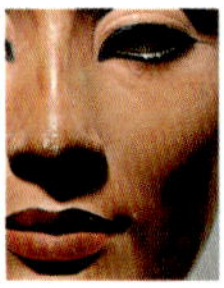

c.1550 BCE

Many royal tombs are built in the Valley of the Kings

1500 to 1332 BCE

The period of the New Kingdom

c.1353–1337 BCE

Reign of Akhenaten, who uses art to emphasize his revolutionary religious views

the region "Akhetaten," which means "the horizon of Aten" and, overturning the certainties of previous ages, Akhenaten and Nefertiti rejected the multiple gods of Egyptian theology in favor of the one all-powerful sun-god, Aten.

Joining her husband in the worship of this new religion, Nefertiti's prominent role in Egyptian royal rule and religious worship reflects her influence in the public sphere. She was often shown making offerings to the Aten and appears to be almost the king's equal in terms of status. Though Akhenaten had several wives, Nefertiti was his favorite and together they had six daughters. Her name roughly translates to "the beautiful one is come." In addition, "nefer" beads were a type of elongated gold bead that she was often portrayed as wearing. Some Egyptologists believe she co-ruled with Akhenaten for some of his reign. In tomb decorations she is depicted wearing the regalia of a pharaoh and sitting on a similar-size throne to Akhenaten. Little is known about her origins but it seems unlikely that she was of royal blood. Her father was possibly a high-ranking royal official called Ay, who went on to become pharaoh after Tutankhamen. After she and Akhenaten died, Egypt reverted to its former religion. This painted limestone bust is the most famous depiction of her. Discovered at Amarna by a team of German archaeologists in 1912, the bust was donated to the Egyptian Museum in Berlin in 1920. Photographs of the bust helped it to attain worldwide iconic status, and it became the most copied work of ancient Egyptian sculpture until Tutankhamen's tomb was discovered a decade later.

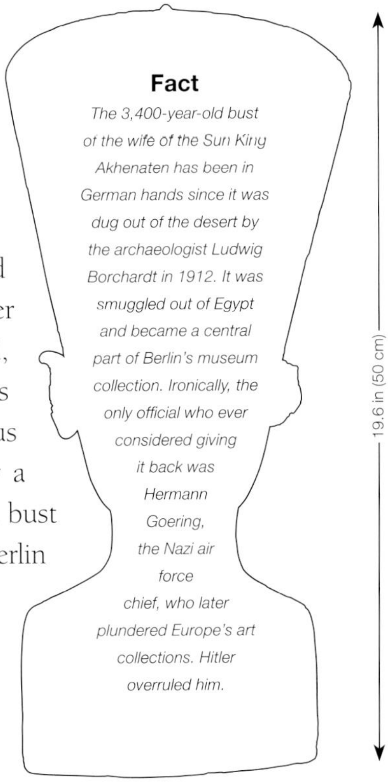

Fact

The 3,400-year-old bust of the wife of the Sun King Akhenaten has been in German hands since it was dug out of the desert by the archaeologist Ludwig Borchardt in 1912. It was smuggled out of Egypt and became a central part of Berlin's museum collection. Ironically, the only official who ever considered giving it back was Hermann Goering, the Nazi air force chief, who later plundered Europe's art collections. Hitler overruled him.

c.1350–1340 BCE	c.1348–c.1339 BCE	1348–1336 BCE	c.1348
The sculptor Tuthmosis creates limestone model of Nefertiti's head and neck	Six daughters are born to Nefertiti and Akhenaten	Akhetaten, Akhenaten's new capital, is built and centered on the new worship of the sun-god Aten	Queen Tiy, Nefertiti's influential mother-in-law, dies in her late 50s

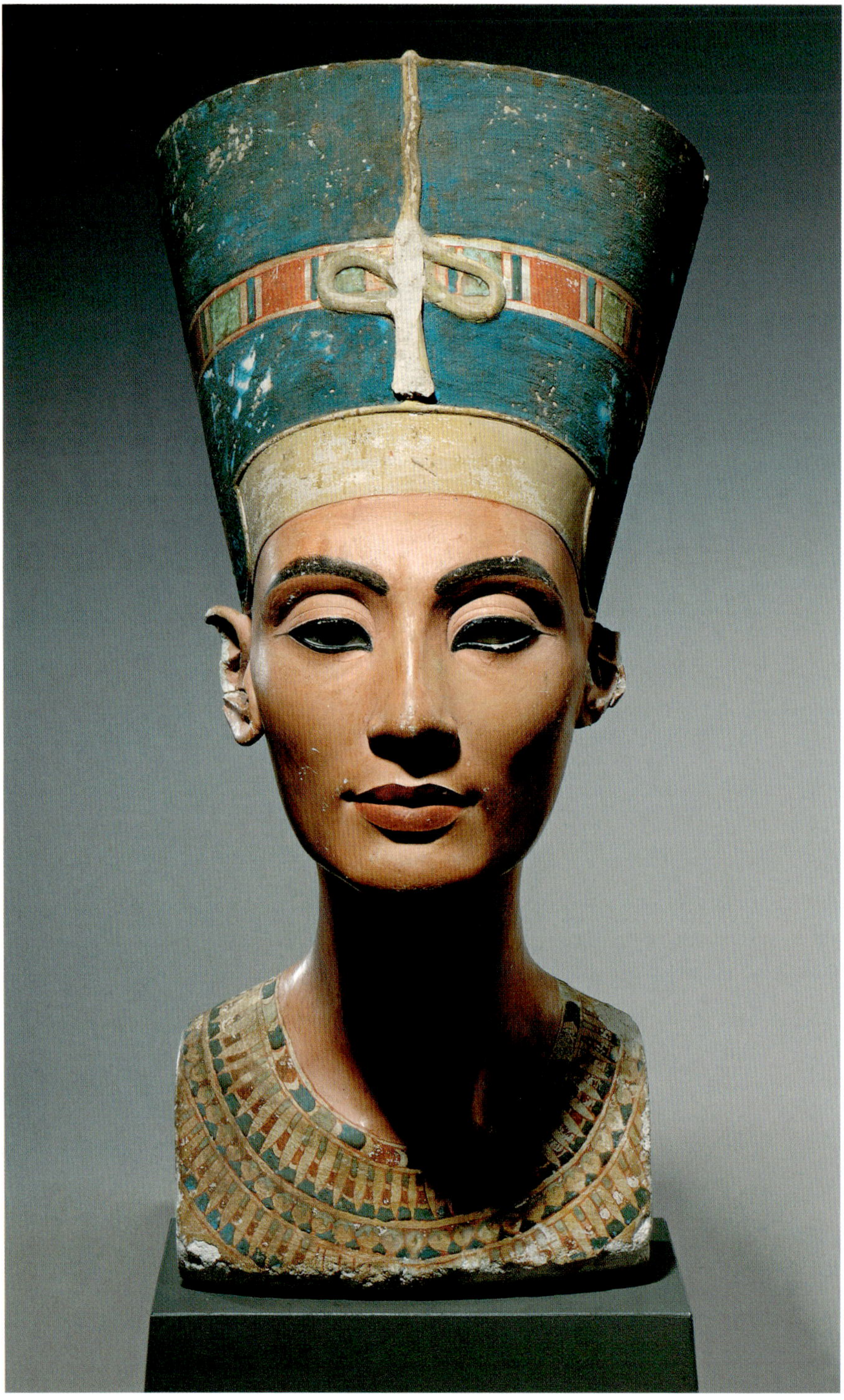

Sculptor Tuthmosis Queen Nefertiti

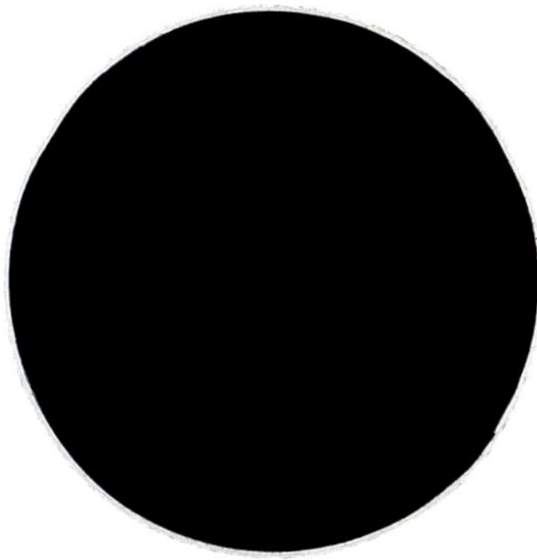

The right eye was a prototype. The students of Tuthmosis needed only to learn to make one eye, so the left eye is missing.

In the New Kingdom, the position of chief sculptors was quite strong. They directed the workmen and sometimes trained apprentices. Sometimes they were priests as well, which isn't as implausible as it might seem. Art was meant to be inspired by the gods and many works were accompanied by religious inscriptions. Although few names have come down to us, we know of Akhenaten's two chief sculptors. Bak was his first and Tuthmosis, the official court sculptor in the second half of Akhenaten's reign, was the creator of Nefertiti's bust. While Nefertiti had previously been depicted with a similar appearance to her husband during Bak's period, under Tuthmosis her features were distinct and individual, showing the more naturalistic approach to art that Akhenaten encouraged.

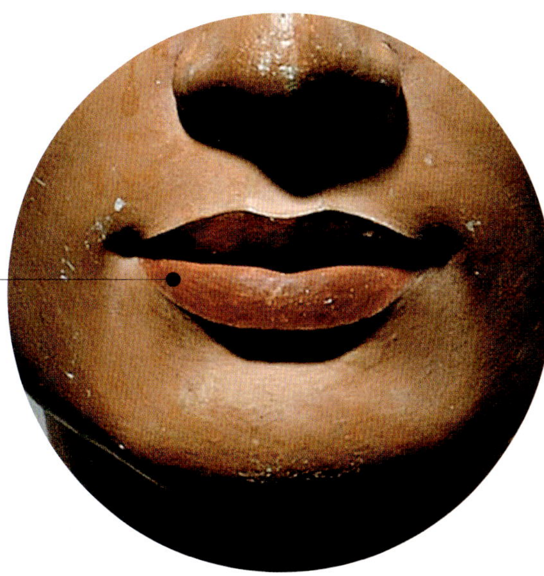

Perfectly carved, Nefertiti's full, red lips, dyed with ocher, reflect the Egyptians' ideals of beauty.

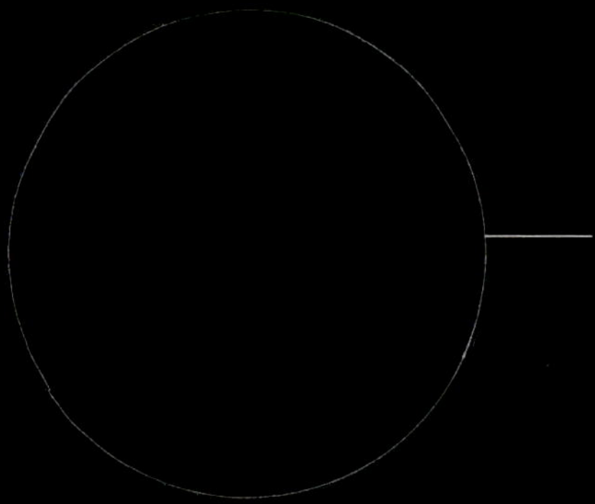

An Egyptian cobra once adorned the crown, enhanced by the blue, red, gold, and green ribbon.

The right eye is neatly inlaid with a piece of pale greenish rock crystal and the pupil is black colored wax.

Tuthmosis painted Nefertiti's skin a flawless pinkish-brown, adding bold red lips and outlining her eyelids and eyebrows in black. Her vibrantly colored necklace of blue, turquoise, red, green, gold, and white contrasts with her skin and blends with her flat-topped blue crown, which is a version of a war crown associated with the goddess Tefnut, who was sometimes called the protector of the sun-god. The paint was water-based and relatively opaque. Pigments have been layered to build up color and it is clear that Tuthmosis has mixed brown with white, yellow, and red, to create the flesh tones.

As Akhenaten's Chief Sculptor and Master of Works, Tuthmosis used color more naturally than his predecessors. His reds were made from iron oxides, yellow from quartz, green was made by corroding copper with vinegar resulting in verdigris, black from soot, and, like others, he made great use of Egyptian blue.

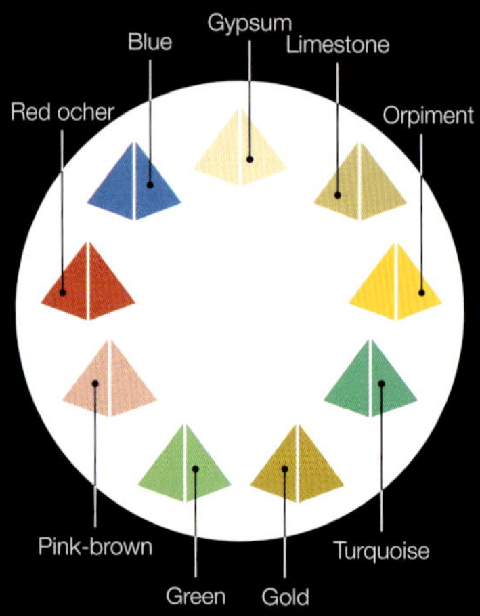

Reflecting the religious revolution Akhenaten initiated, Tuthmosis developed a subtle style combined with careful attention to detail, instilling his portraits with grace and sensitivity.

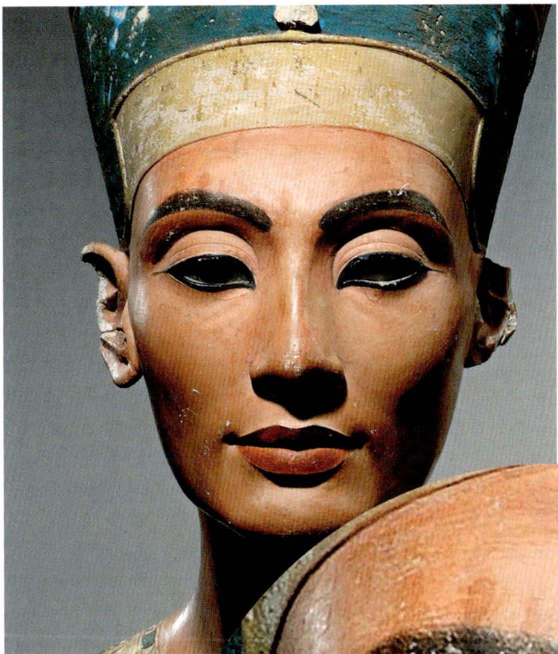

In the traditional manner, Tuthmosis used bronze tools to make this bust but he flouted convention when he taught his craftsmen and apprentices to work in a more lifelike manner. The statue's timeless beauty was intended to weave a spell to enforce eternal life.

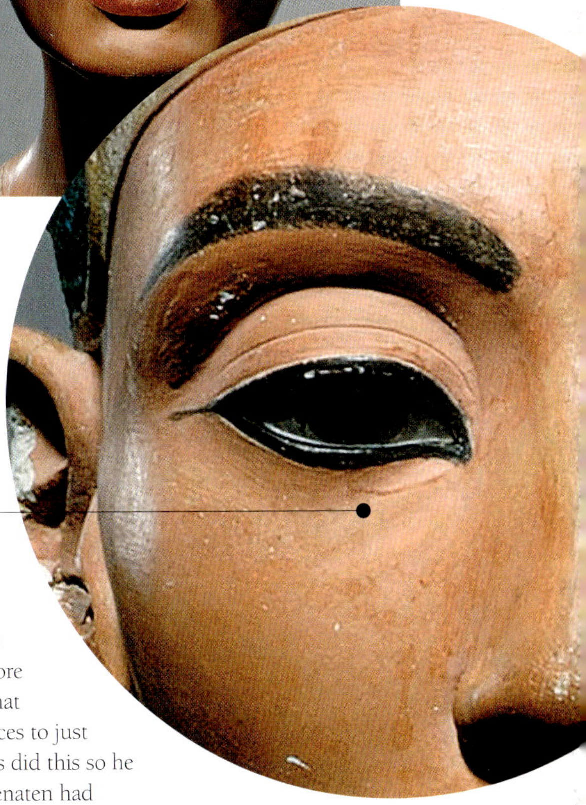

There is some wrinkling around Nefertiti's eyes and on her neck. The plaster was shaped to replicate the fine lines under the queen's eyes and on her neck, a level of detail that other Egyptian art simply did not include.

Once thought to be painted limestone, it is now believed that the bust is a limestone core covered with a layer of plaster or gypsum that ranges from $1\frac{1}{2}$ in/4 cm thick in some places to just $\frac{1}{32}$ in /1 mm on Nefertiti's face. Tuthmosis did this so he could adjust the model as he worked. Akhenaten had instructed him to represent what he saw and this is why the Nefertiti bust seems so realistic. The elongated neck, almond-shape eyes, high cheekbones, slender nose, and plump lips have given her the reputation of being one of the most beautiful women who ever lived, but Egyptian art can never be taken literally.

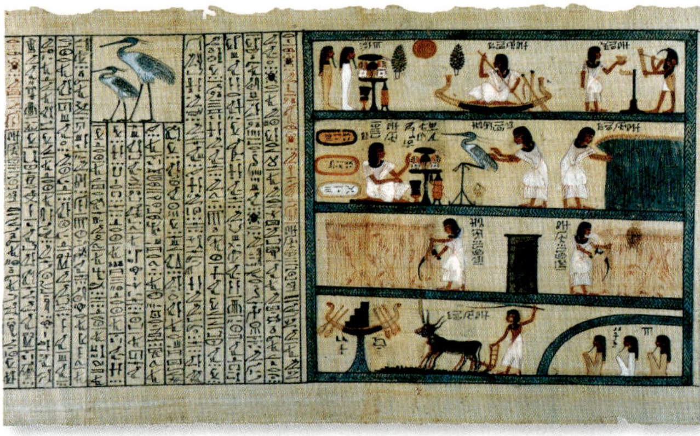

ORIGINALLY FROM THE TOMB OF NAKHT, THEBES,
NOW IN THE BRITISH MUSEUM, LONDON

The Papyrus of Nakht from the Book of the Dead

Pigment on papyrus,
c.1350–1300 BCE

Throughout the Old and Middle kingdoms, all wealthy people made preparations for the afterlife, although royalty, because they were considered to be gods, had more ornate arrangements.

The Book of the Dead (named by Egyptologists) was an important part of any tomb because it described many of the spells needed to reach the afterlife and included hymns praising various gods. The earliest spells like this were inscribed on pyramid walls, called the Pyramid Texts, and some were also found on walls of tombs and on coffins, or written on linen or vellum. Later on, adaptations were written on a papyrus, rolled up and placed in the coffin or burial chamber of the deceased. These were covered with magical texts and

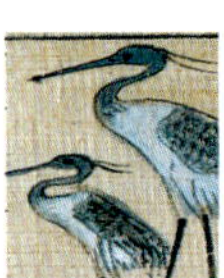

1347 BCE

King Erechtheus II of Athens is reportedly killed by lightning after a reign of 50 years

1346 BCE

Amenhotep IV begins his cult of Aten and the construction of Amarna as his new capital

1345 BCE

Amenhotep IV changes his name to Akhenaten

accompanying illustrations called vignettes, and some of the finest examples were made during the late 18th and early 19th dynasties of the New Kingdom. Although most Books of the Dead were written for men and the text often reflects this, there are a few known cases made for women.

The spells and texts primarily served to provide for and protect the deceased, helping them to pass through the dangerous underworld on the way to the afterlife. Huge changes were made to the spells over time and later in Egyptian history the more ritualistic parts of the text disappeared completely, although most spells remained fundamentally the same. There were also changes made if the priests at the time preferred a particular god—that god would appear more often in the vignettes. Altogether, nearly 200 individual spells have been found, although no one papyrus contains them all.

Wealthy Egyptians commissioned scribes to produce their personal selection of spells and to paint individual vignettes featuring themselves. The less wealthy could buy preprepared templates, in which blank spaces had been left for the insertion of the client's name. Nakht was a royal scribe and military commander at the end of the 18th and beginning of the 19th dynasties. The skill and individualism in his Book of the Dead show how wealthy and high-ranking he was during life.

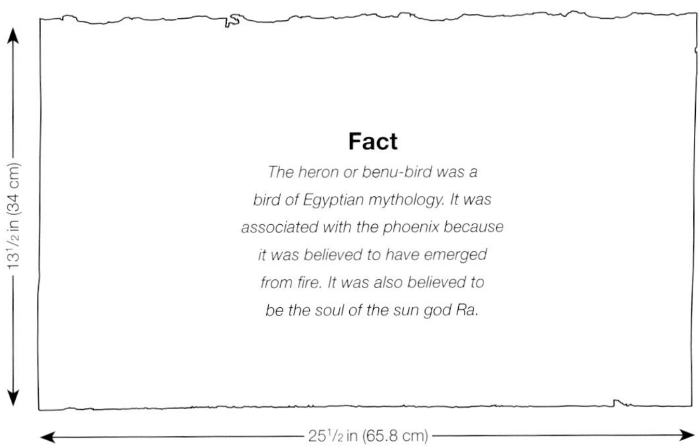

Fact

The heron or benu-bird was a bird of Egyptian mythology. It was associated with the phoenix because it was believed to have emerged from fire. It was also believed to be the soul of the sun god Ra.

c.1341/1340 BCE

Tutankhaten, later Tutankhamen, pharaoh of Egypt, is born

c.1340 BCE

Citadel walls are built in Mycenae

1340 BCE

Civil war in Mitanni—a kingdom in northern Mesopotamia

1320 BCE

End of the 18th and start of the 19th dynasty of the New Kingdom

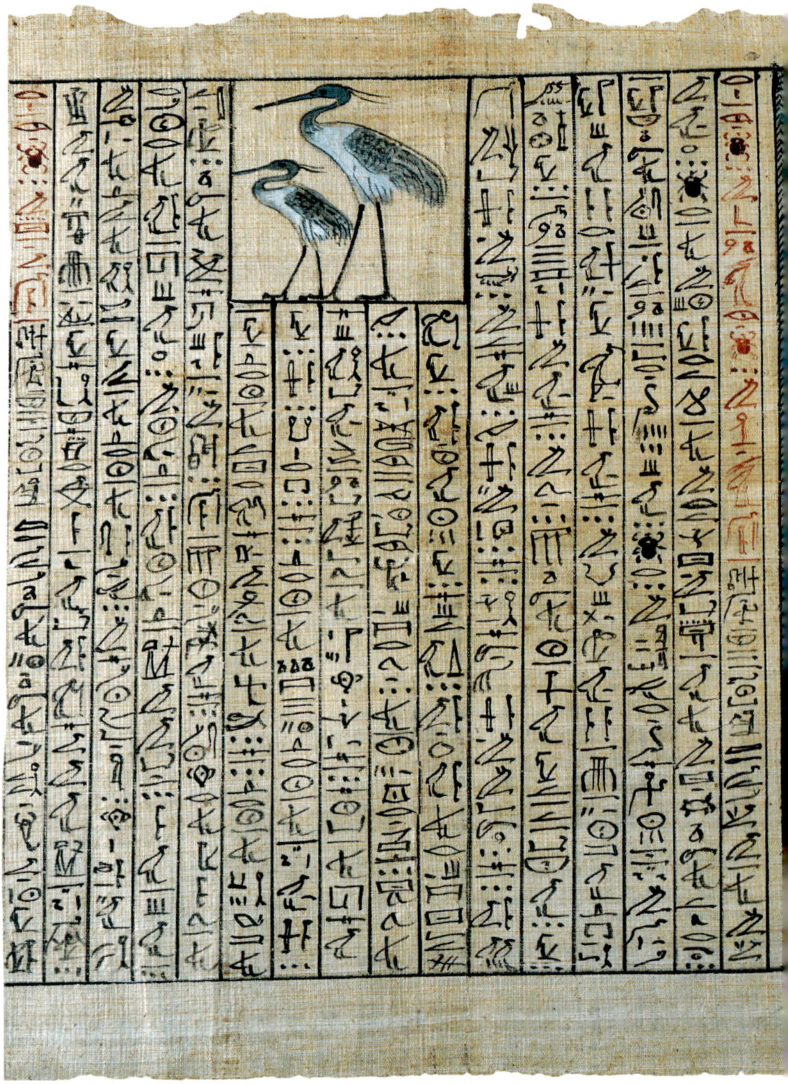

This papyrus shows Spell 110, which was aimed at the gods who live in the Field of Offering and the Field of Rushes—both in the afterlife. The deceased was expected to undertake agricultural work in the Field of Rushes. The paintings show areas of land surrounded by water. At the top right, Nakht is accompanied by ibis-headed Thoth, with the scales and the feather of Maat, referring to the Judgment Scene (*see pages 86–91*). He then paddles his boat across the Lake of Offerings where two mummified gods stand before a table of offerings. On the section below, Nakht worships the benu-bird and, in the following spaces, he is portrayed pulling flax, reaping, and plowing. The boat of Wennefer (another name for Osiris), who is shown with the head of a snake, is moored in a channel of the water at the bottom. Three gods from the ennead

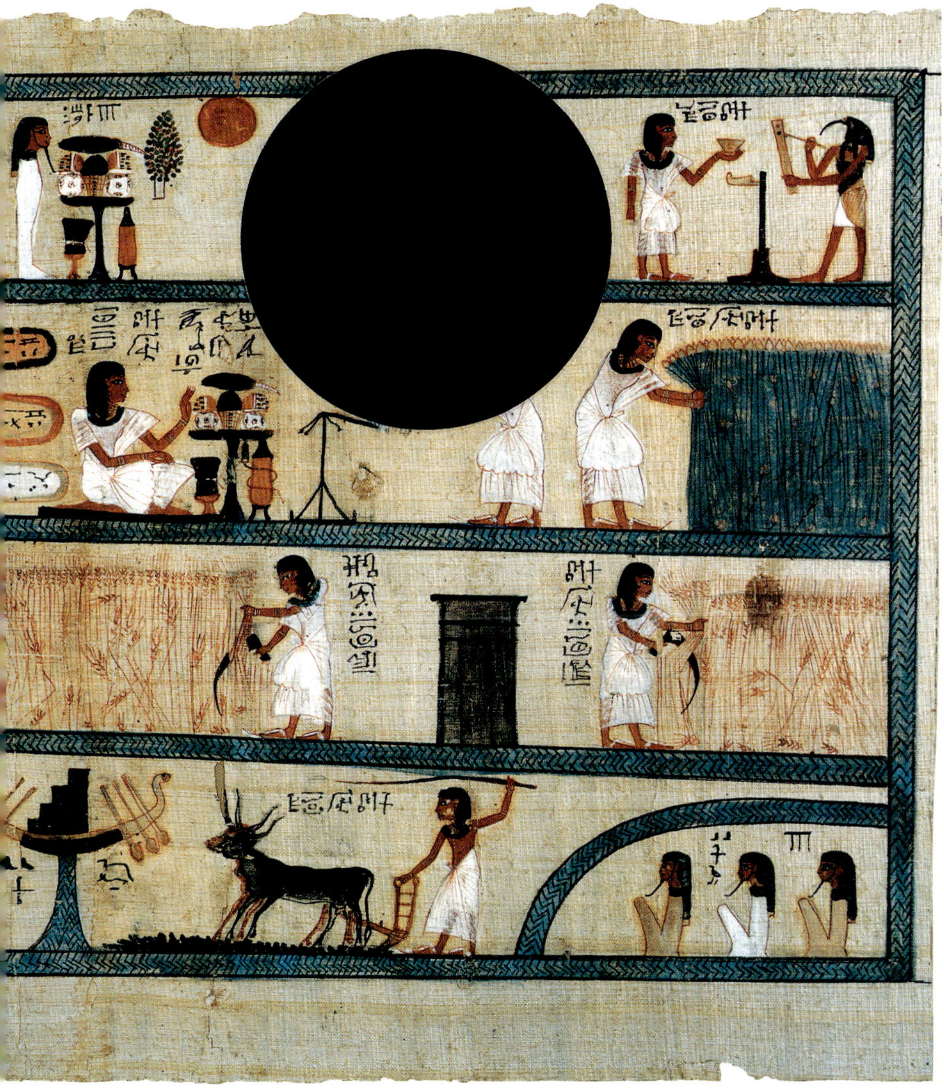

(a group of nine gods) are shown at the bottom right. Intentionally, the papyrus reads like a story in a comic book. Vignettes were always placed at the beginning of the text (papyri were read from right to left) to illustrate the spell or ritual. The traditionally simplistic portrayal was believed to be the only way such representations could be brought to life and every relevant action had to be depicted as clearly as possible, explaining clearly what was happening to both the deceased and the relevant gods. Simplicity was essential to describe each action Nakht has to undertake for a successful pathway through the Fields of Rushes and Offering. Incidentally, throughout the entire papyrus, Nakht is portrayed wearing the funerary white linen or lawn pleated costume.

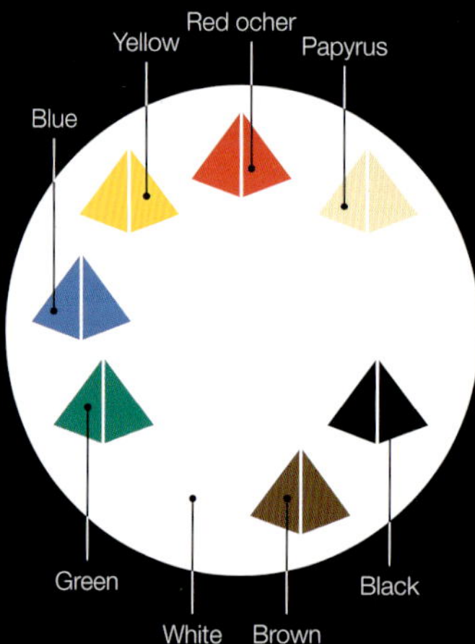

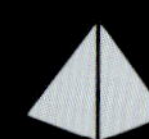

These herons represent the sacred Egyptian benu-bird, believed to be the soul of the sun god Ra. The benu-bird was always painted as gray, purple, blue, or white, with a long beak and a two-feathered crest.

Papyrus is made from pressed reeds and can become damaged over time. It was used for everyday writing, but also for documents that were put in the tomb alongside the dead. Scribes wrote hieratic script (a cursive form of ancient Egyptian writing that lost the pictorial aspect of hieroglyphs) quickly, using ink with a reed brush on papyrus.

Although transparency was considered bad practice in painting, this artist has used it skillfully to describe materials, a technique virtually unseen before the Amarna period. For instance, Nakht's legs and shoulders can be seen through his white overrobe, showing the lightness of the fabric. It was not easy to achieve translucency with the chalky and dense pigments available. Scribes, using reed pens and ink, and artists, using paint and brushes, worked on this document together. The two professions were often interlinked. While hieroglyphs were only ever written in black or red, vignettes were allowed a greater selection of colors. The green used here was probably malachite (copper carbonate); the white was gypsum, and the yellow, red, and brown made from iron oxide.

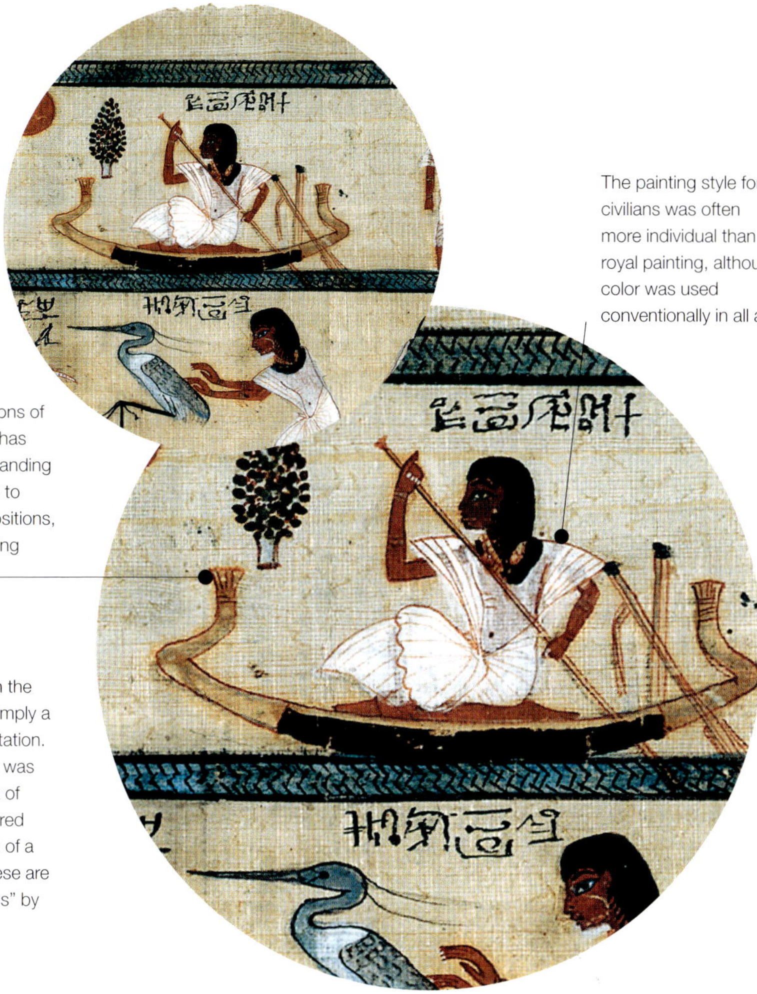

The painting style for civilians was often more individual than royal painting, although color was used conventionally in all art.

In the eight versions of Nakht, the artist has used his understanding of human figures to create natural positions, instead of following tradition.

Black outlines on the vignettes were simply a style of representation. In the text, black was used for the bulk of the writing while red showed the start of a new subject. These are known as "rubrics" by Egyptologists.

To enable the paint to spread evenly and flow through reed pens, dry, finely ground pigments were mixed with water. Artists and scribes also mixed very small quantities of organic materials to make the pigment stick to the papyrus. In the main, these were plant gums although they have proved difficult to analyze because they are only present in tiny amounts. The style of the art had by now returned essentially to the conventional and traditional methods of the preAmarna period, but some slight stylistic changes were left over from that time. The combination of geometric regularity and keen observation of nature was adhered to but, along with the compressing of human proportions, an intimacy and almost personal touch crept in.

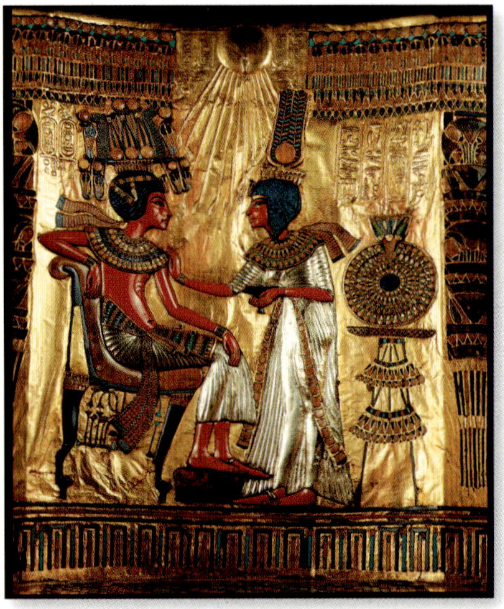

FROM THE VALLEY OF THE KINGS, THEBES, NOW IN THE EGYPTIAN MUSEUM, CAIRO

Golden Throne of Tutankhamen

Wood, gold, faience, colored glass, lapis lazuli, calcite, 18th dynasty, c.1330 BCE

UNTIL TUTANKHAMEN'S TOMB WAS DISCOVERED in 1922, he was one of the least known of the pharaohs. Perhaps because it was prepared in a hurry, his was unlike other royal tombs, consisting of only four small rooms rather than the long corridor that was typical of the time. Born in Akhetaten during the Amarna period, it is probable that Tutankhamen was Akhenaten's son by another queen —not Nefertiti. It is recorded that Akhenaten and Nefertiti had six daughters. Tutankhamen was soon married to one of these daughters, Ankhesenamun (*see*

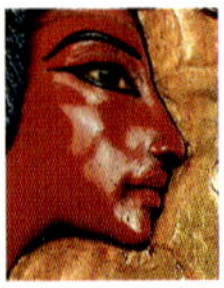

c.1348–1324 BCE

Lifespan of Ankhesenamun, daughter of Akhenaten, who marries Tutankhamen

1344–1322 BCE

Beginning of the Hittite Empire in Anatolia (Turkey)

c.1336–1327 BCE

Reign of Tutankhamen and return to Thebes as capital of Egypt

page 75). Marriage to a woman of the royal line was helpful to ensure that Tutankhamen fitted even more strongly into the royal line, and it was commonplace to marry one's close relation (his father married one of his daughters, for instance). First known as Tutankhaten, he changed his name to Tutankhamen on the insistence of his advisors, presumably to try to distance himself from the Atenist theories of Akhenaten.

This gilded and inlaid chair was found in a small room off the main antechamber of the tomb, along with other magnificent items of furniture, including beds, chests, stools, and more thrones. It shows some particularly advanced techniques in the craft of furniture making. As well as their ability in working precious metals and inlays, the Egyptians were also skilled woodworkers. Many of today's craftsmen would have difficulty matching the finely embellished details and overall quality of the construction of this chair. Its style—it has an inlaid and illustrated back—was popular for royal chairs of the 18th dynasty. The composition on the back of the chair, which shows the king with Ankhesenamun, demonstrates the legacy of the informal style of Amarna. The young queen is anointing her husband with perfumed oil from a vessel—as was the custom to ensure his eternal life. As she performs this ritual, the Aten disk with its rays ending in small hands and ankhs (the ankh—a looped iron—is a sign of eternal life) radiates its blessing on the royal couple. The iconography relates back to Akhenaten, and the names of the king and queen carved on the chair use both the earlier (Aten) and later (Amen) forms, showing that they lived during a period of transition from Amarna back to traditional Egyptian art and beliefs.

Fact

It is debatable whether the throne was first commissioned for Akhenaten and later altered for Tutankhamen, or whether it was produced early in Tutankhamen's reign during the transition back to the orthodox religion.

21 in (53 cm)

20 in (51 cm)

c.1332 to 1085 BCE

Thebes is restored as capital of Egypt for the remainder of the New Kingdom

1331 BCE

Tutankhaten renames himself Tutankhamen and returns to Thebes from Amarna

c.1324–1320 BCE

Ay, although born a commoner, becomes pharaoh after the death of Tutankhamen

1320 BCE

End of the 18th dynasty of the New Kingdom in Egypt

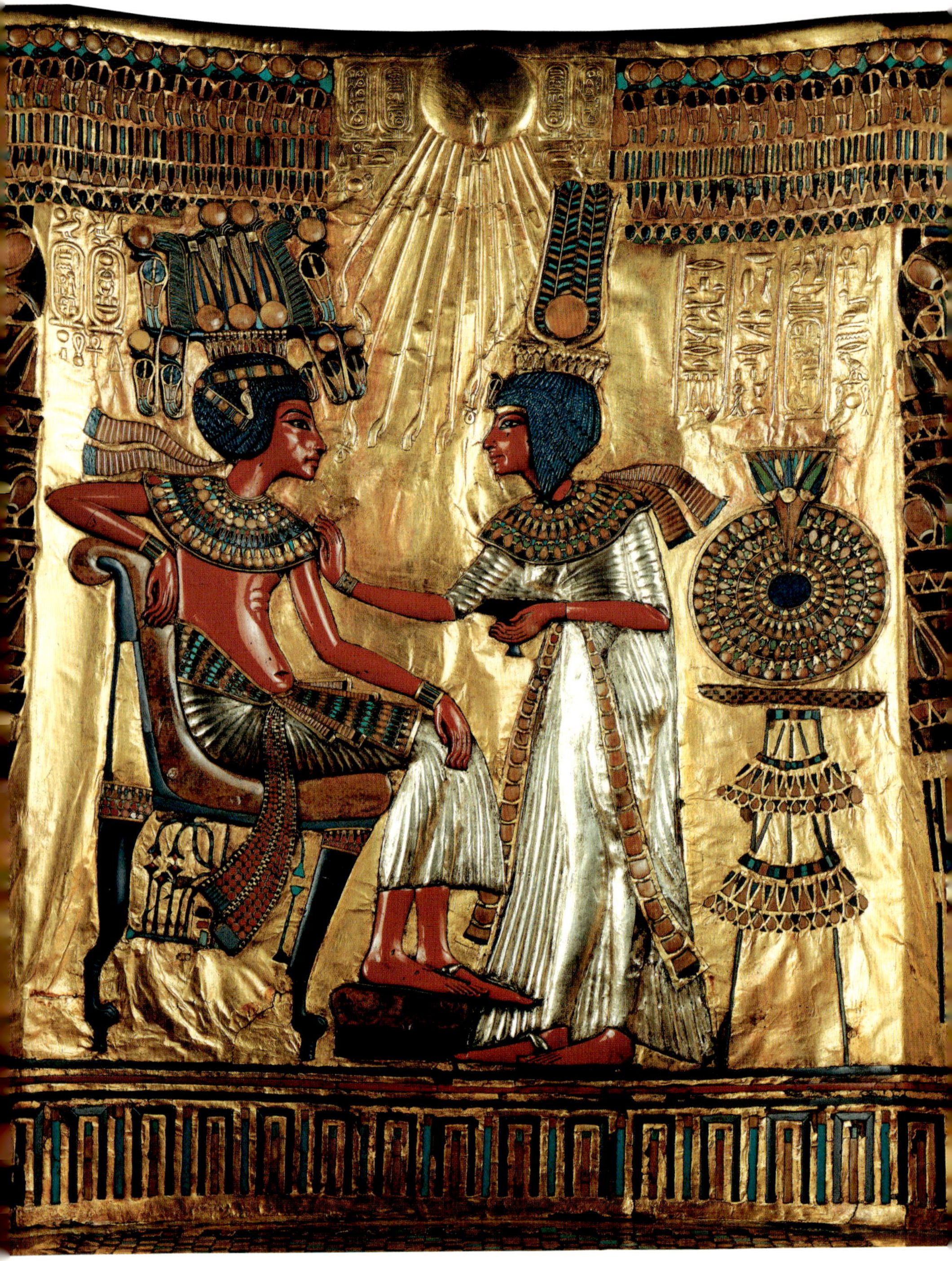

he throne. Elsewhere it is abundant in animal
ation, while the actual back represents the king
ral pose. The throne back was designed on a
ving artistic and religious practices, ensuring a
on. Amarna's ideas remained influential, which
royal couple's naturally affectionate relationship
the Aten confidently shines over the figures of
ueen Ankhesenum.

Tutankhamen faces right and Ankhesenamun faces left as convention dictated. Behind Tutankhamen are two of his cartouches, lozenge-shaped signs used as symbols of protection around his name.

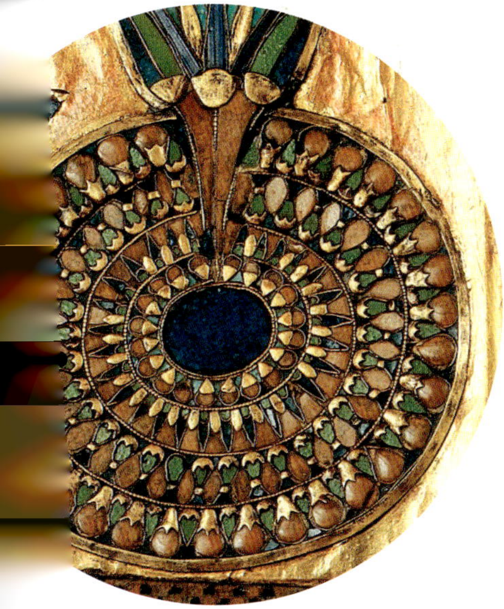

Carved in wood, the throne is covered in sheet gold with some silver overlay. Colored glass, faience, calcite, and semiprecious stones embellish it. The bodies and wigs are inlaid with specially made red and blue glass.

The color of the sky and lifegiving water, blue was also linked with gods. Most gods had blue hair and Amun had a blue face.

Ankhesenum's double feather crown of ostrich
represented truth, order, justice, and freedom, a
the middle stood for life and light. Tutankhame
has a base of protective cobras, two feathers, an
elements, like the crown of the underworld dei
cobras, each with a blazing sun disk on its heac
of the crown. Copper is used quite extensively
Minerals containing deposits of copper include
azurite (blue), cuprite (red), and turquoise (bl
was easily melted down to obtain the copper;
because the Egyptians associated it with rebirt
ground copper in the faience process used her
glazing objects made from silica and firing the
these pieces developed a shiny blue-green pati
inlays are also made with copper.

Specialist tools were used to depress the soft gold and then semiprecious stones and colored glass were bonded in position.

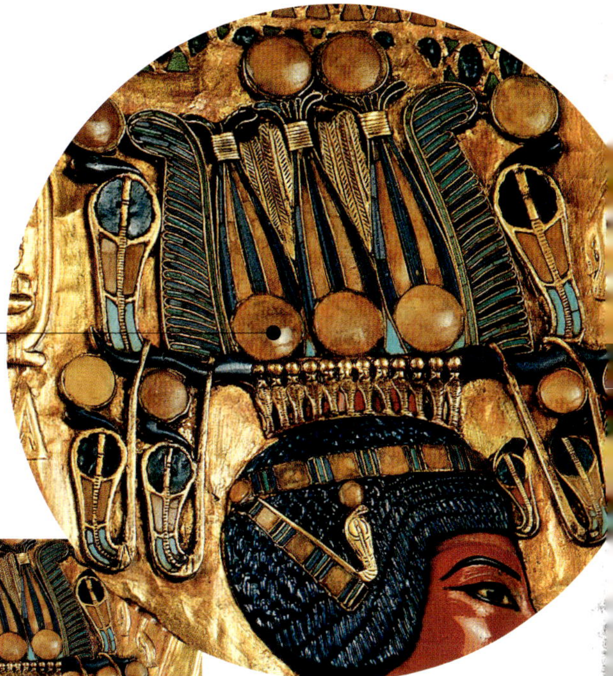

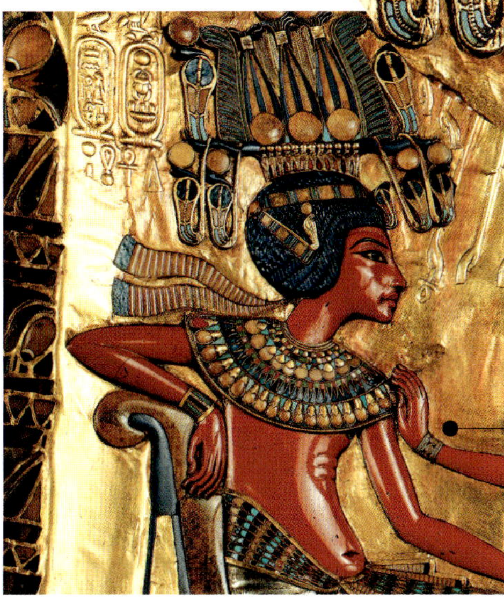

Gold was mined from the Eastern Desert, Nubia, and Syria-Palestine. The Egyptians' wealth in gold made them the envy of their neighbors.

Traditional Egyptian art was all about eternity, while the art of Amarna existed more for the moment and reveled in the world created and governed by the sun. This throne bridges the two types of art, celebrating both the now and the hereafter.

The makers of this throne created a symbolic and decorative scene within a balanced design. Gold was the main material and each stone or piece of glass told a story. The royal couple are in a floral pavilion while the rays of the Aten disk enter through an opening in the roof. Details, such as the bodies, jewelry, hair, crowns, the trim of their garments, and the furniture, are created with glass and semiprecious stones in colors that mirror the paints used in wall paintings and that have connections with individual gods. The garments are finely pleated, white linen, and sandals are rendered in chased silver, which was a rare metal in Egypt and believed to be the substance of gods' bones.

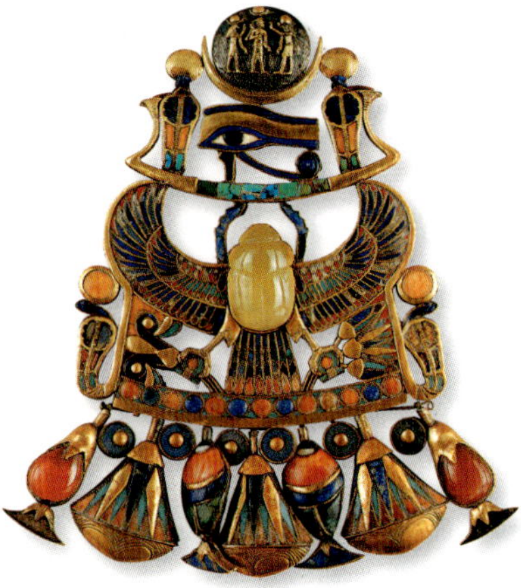

FROM THE TOMB OF TUKANKHAMEN, VALLEY OF THE KINGS, THEBES, CURRENTLY IN THE EGYPTIAN MUSEUM, CAIRO

Winged Scarab Pendant

Cloisonné, gold, silver, chalcedony, semi-precious stones including lapis lazuli and turquoise, colored glass, c.1330 BCE

THIS IS ONE OF THE ITEMS OF JEWELRY FOUND in the tomb of Tutankhamen. Pendants of this type were not made simply for their decorative appearance; the collection of signs and symbols were combined to create a magical object or charm that the pharaoh wore as a kind of talisman. Most wealthy Egyptians wore amulets of some kind for protection or good luck and everyone knew what each god, symbolic shape, material, or color represented. For example, blue was for protection, the bull or lion attracted courage, and the ankh was a symbol of life itself. To us, the necklace is aesthetically pleasing, but to the Egyptians, the entire object had a miraculous aura.

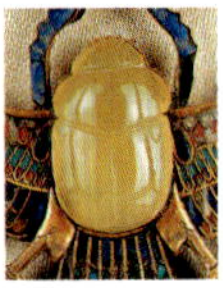

c.1345 BCE

Kiya, the second wife of Akhenaten, possibly gives birth to the future Tutankhamen

c.1340 BCE

Temple art and architecture revert to original worship of Osiris and all other Egyptian gods

1338–1336 BCE

An ephemeral figure, Smenkhkara, is thought to have ruled alongside Akhenaten

By far the most important amulet in ancient Egypt was the scarab, symbolically as sacred to the Egyptians as the cross is to Christians. Scarab dung beetles lay eggs in a pellet, which they roll along, and the Egyptians regarded this action as an image of the sun and its course through the heavens, rolled by a gigantic beetle. So scarabs are associated with the Egyptian god Khepri, who pushed the sun across the sky. Each day the sun disappeared, always to rise again and be reborn the following day and, as a result, the scarab beetle became an ancient Egyptian symbol for rebirth. They were worn as jewelry and amulets. The Heart Scarab had hieroglyphic inscriptions on the back and was often buried over the heart of the dead to ensure the rebirth in the afterlife.

In this pendant, the central element is a winged scarab, but every other part of it is symbolic too. This scarab has the wings and tail of a falcon and in its claws it holds a shen ring that symbolized eternity. Also in its claws are a sacred blue lotus and a papyrus flower, which were symbols of Upper and Lower Egypt, the sun, and creation. Above, supported by its front legs and wing tips, is a gold barque (boat), its hull inlaid with turquoise. The barque signified the River Nile, Egypt's lifeline. The gods determined the height of the annual Nile floods and so it depended on them whether there would be a good harvest or a famine.

Fact

The shen ring represented the concept of eternity. Like a wedding ring, it has no beginning or end, and the filled center of the shen circle symbolizes the sun disk.

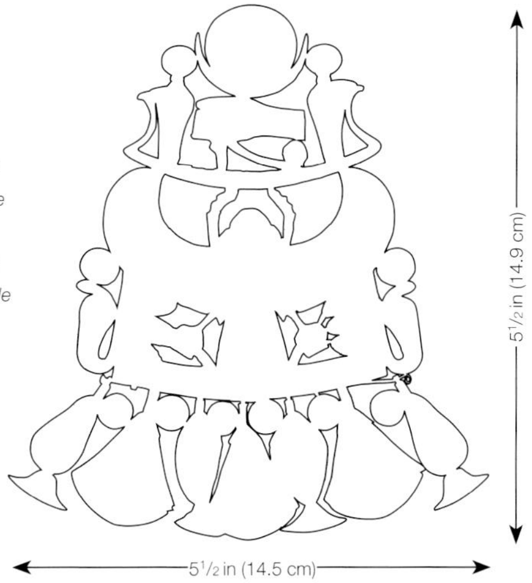

c.1337 BCE

Carved figures of Nefertiti replace winged goddesses at the corners of Akhenaten's sarcophagus

1336–1327

Throughout Tutankhamen's reign, Akhenaten's temples remain standing

c.1332 BCE

Horemheb, Tutankhamen's commander, is named regent, should the King die without issue

c.1330 BCE

Most important document of Tutankhamen's reign, the Restoration Stele, criticizes Akhenaten's reforms

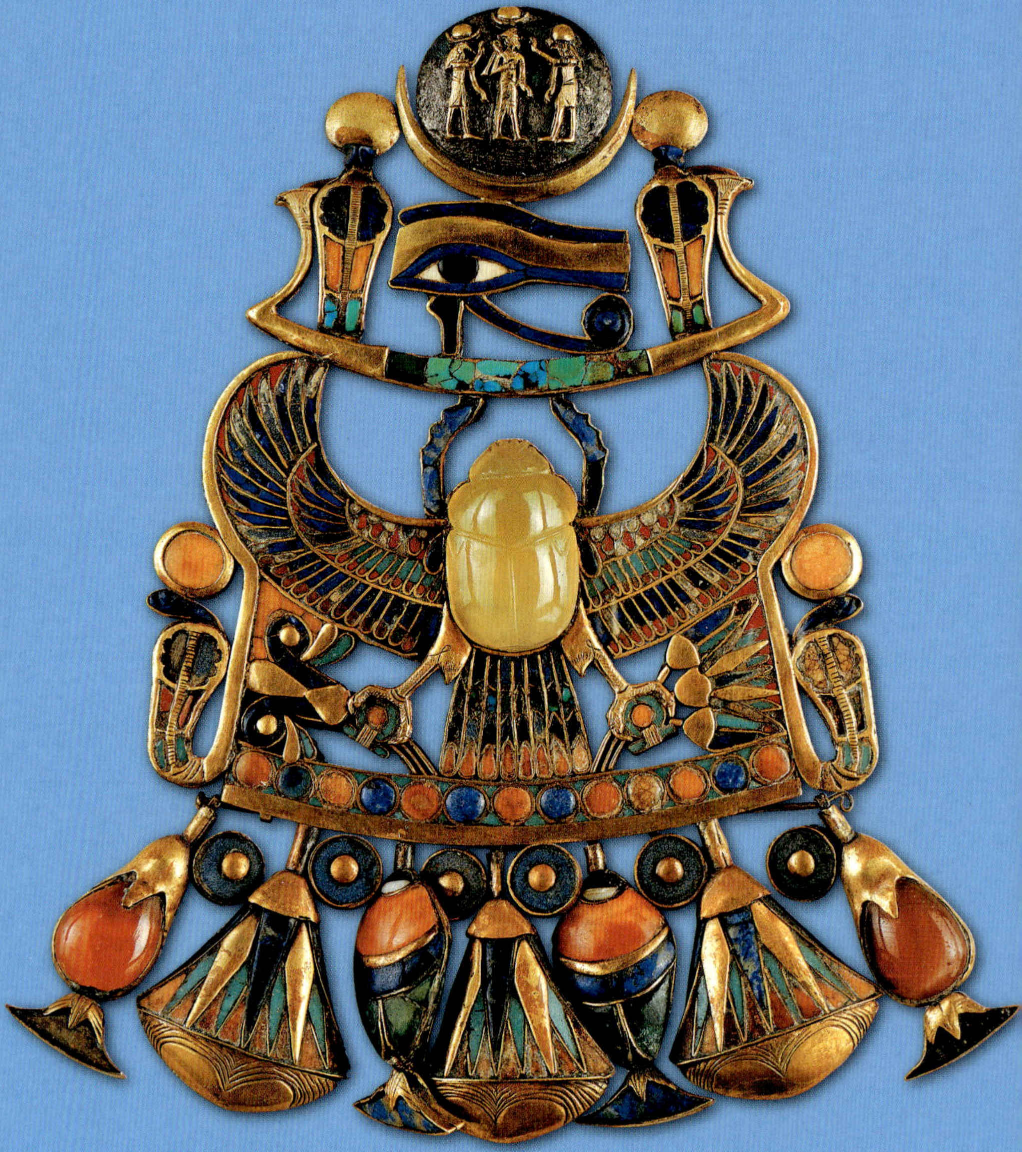

Above the udjat eye is a lunar crescent of gold, and a silver disk displaying the gods Thoth and Re-Horakhty crowning the pharaoh.

Two cobras on the barque flank the eye of Horus (known as the udjat). They symbolize Wadjet, the goddess of Lower Egypt.

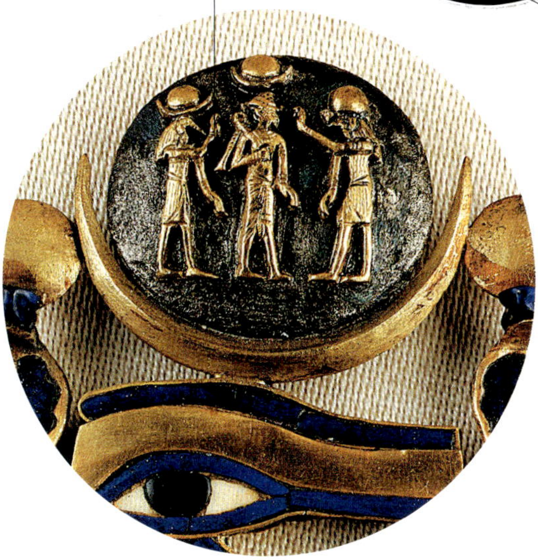

The quality of execution of Egyptian jewelry is outstanding. Like many of the items in Tutankhamen's tomb, this intricately designed pendant reflects aspects of the traditional religion that the young king restored. It was found in a box in the Treasury with other similar objects, probably all of which were originally from Tutankhamen's personal collection of jewelry. The entire object was believed to be imbued with particular protective powers that warded off evil. Most scarab amulets were made for the living. In Egyptian symbolism the sun god could be represented both as a scarab and as a falcon and composite forms of two related symbols were common. This scarab has the forelegs of a scarab and gold falcon's legs.

The udjat was always depicted as a blue or green human eye and eyebrow and decorated with markings of falcon's eyes.

The pendant displays some impressive cloisonné technique that originated in Egypt around 1800 BCE Glass and semiprecious stones are held in position by delicate strips of gold soldered to the gold base. Everything, from the cobras to the scarab wings, is outlined in gold.

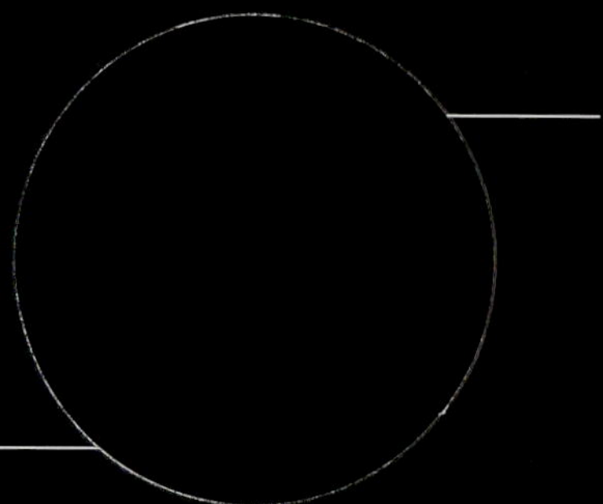

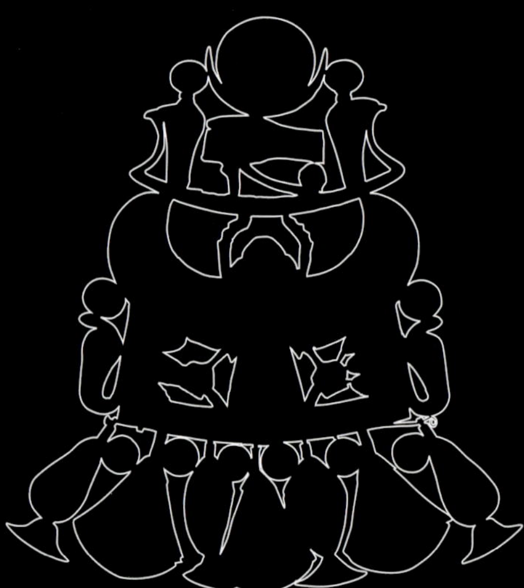

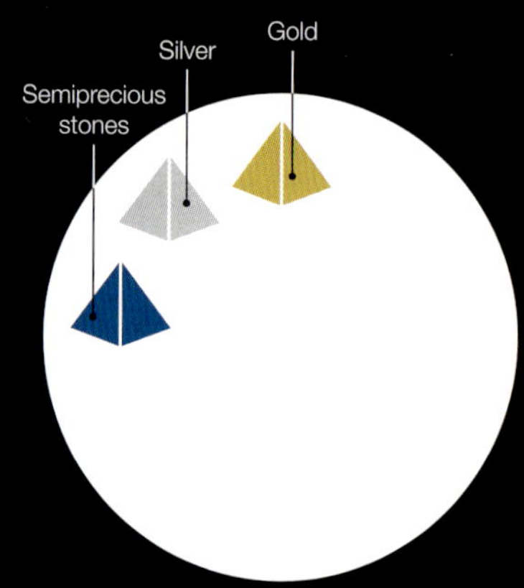

The belief in the potency of these charms to protect their owner and provide the good things in this life as well as the next is evidenced by the craftsmanship. The majority of scarabs were small and made in a wide variety of materials, such as carnelian, lapis lazuli, turquoise, colored glass, faience (glazed composite of silica and quartz) or steatite ("soapstone,") and alabaster. The art of goldsmithing reached its peak in the Middle Kingdom, when Egyptian craftsmen mastered the technical methods required to produce complex items of jewelry. During the New Kingdom, goldsmithing flourished as never before because of regular missions to the Eastern Desert and Nubia to extract metals. Blue lotus and papyrus flowers fringe the base of the pendant, projecting from poppy buds and separated by circles.

The ancient Egyptian word for turquoise was *mefkat*, which meant joy or delight; gold as the color of the sun symbolized eternity and constancy and blue represented the blue of the lifegiving River Nile and the unending sky.

In comparison with other artists, the status of jewelers was low. They labored in dirty, hot conditions, yet their skills were diverse and painstaking. In addition, they had to know the significance of every stone, metal, and piece of glass.

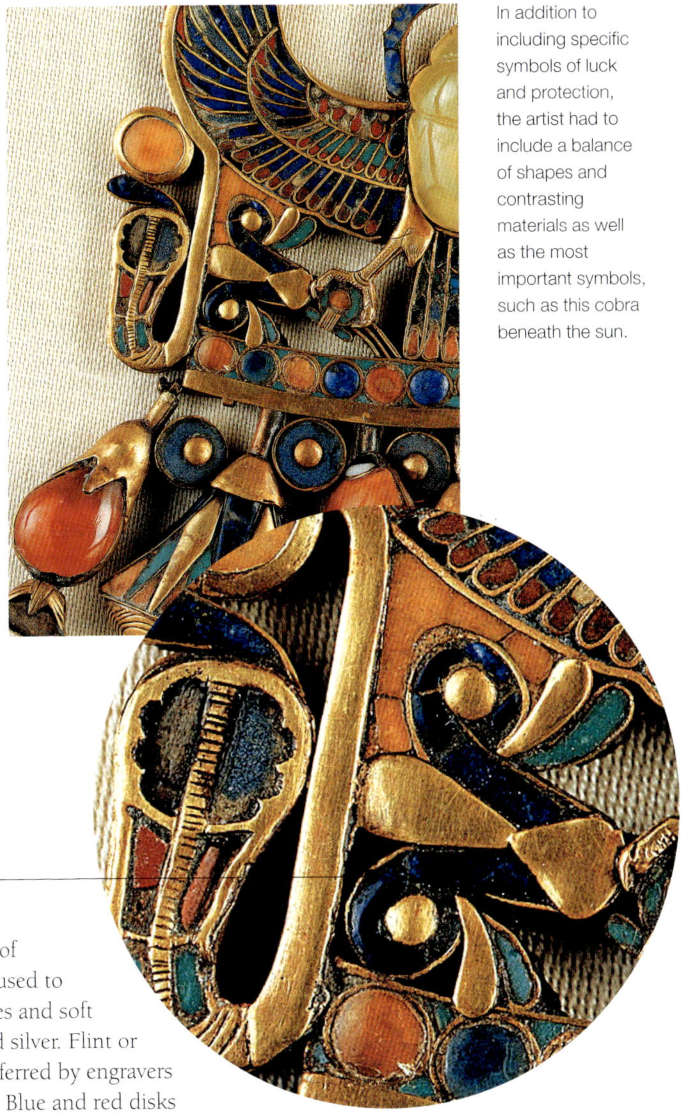

In addition to including specific symbols of luck and protection, the artist had to include a balance of shapes and contrasting materials as well as the most important symbols, such as this cobra beneath the sun.

Along with cloisonné, Egyptian craftsmen invented enameling—seen here, where metals, glass, and semiprecious stones were fused together with melted glass.

During this time, tools of hardened bronze were used to fashion both hard stones and soft metals such as gold and silver. Flint or obsidian tools were preferred by engravers of delicate inscriptions. Blue and red disks stretching from one cobra to the other beneath the winged scarab were made with a glass-fusing technique where glass was heated to melting point so it amalgamated with other materials. Ancient Egyptian glass was tinted with pigments added to the raw glass. Red or orange was produced with oxides of copper, greenish blue (in imitation of the prized turquoise) was made using copper or iron compounds, and dark blue (in imitation of lapis lazuli) was formed using cobalt compounds.

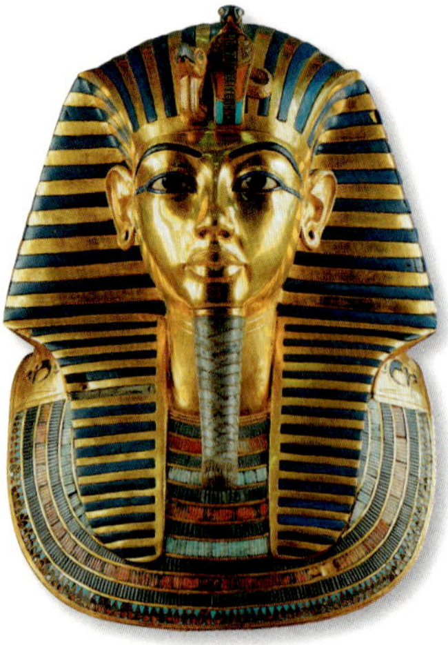

FROM THE VALLEY OF THE KINGS, THEBES, NOW IN THE EGYPTIAN MUSEUM, CAIRO

Funerary Mask of Tutankhamen

Gold inlaid with colored glass and semiprecious stones, c.1323 BCE

THE ULTIMATE IN HIDDEN TREASURE, this gleaming death mask of King Tutankhamen comes from his mummy. Weighing about 24 pounds (11 kg), the mask was placed over the head and shoulders of Tutankhamen's mummy, outside the linen bandages in which his whole body was wrapped. At just nine years old, Tutankhamen became the twelfth pharaoh of the 18th dynasty of Egypt, during the New Kingdom. He died when he was about 19 years old; his death is believed to have been from a swift attack of gangrene after breaking his leg. The mask was made after his death by Egyptian craftsmen and was found in 1922 by British archaeologist Howard Carter in the

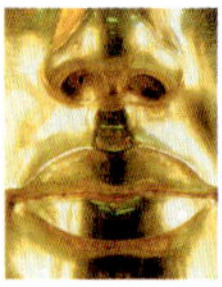

1352 BCE

Amenhotep IV, later known as Akhenaten, ascends the throne of Egypt

1336 BCE

Akhenaten's rule ends, but the distinctive art of his reign continues

1335 BCE

Aged nine, Tutankhamen is crowned pharaoh and restores worship of traditional gods

Valley of the Kings. The tomb of Tutankhamen is the only fully intact Egyptian tomb that has ever been found, and has enlightened Egyptologists and mesmerized the rest of us ever since.

Tutankhamen's background is uncertain. An inscription calls him a king's son, but it is unclear which king was meant. Some believe that Amenhotep III was possibly his father and others believe that he was either the son or the younger brother of Akhenaten. After Akhenaten's death, he became king and married Akhenaten's third daughter to strengthen his claim to the throne. For nearly 10 years he ruled Egypt, changing his name from Tutankhaten—meaning "Living Image of Aten," to Tutankhamen—meaning "Living Image of Amun." He is famous, not for great deeds or discoveries, but because of the wealth of art, jewels, and other magnificent artifacts found in his tomb. The mask was intended to protect the young pharaoh on his way to the afterlife. The vulture goddess Nekhbet and cobra goddess Wadjet on the forehead, as well as the falcon heads on the shoulders of the mask, were symbols of Upper and Lower Egypt and of divine authority. All pharaohs after Mentuhotep II in 2061–2010 BCE used these symbols for protection and to show that they ruled both parts of Egypt. An inscription engraved on the shoulders and on the back of the mask is a spell that first appeared on masks of the Middle Kingdom, about 500 years before Tutankhamen's reign.

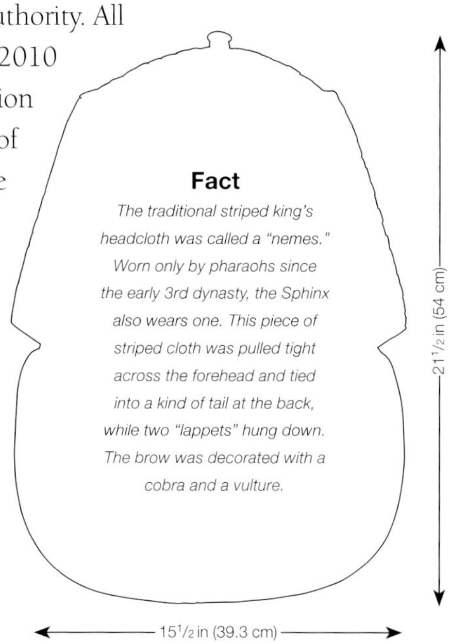

Fact

The traditional striped king's headcloth was called a "nemes." Worn only by pharaohs since the early 3rd dynasty, the Sphinx also wears one. This piece of striped cloth was pulled tight across the forehead and tied into a kind of tail at the back, while two "lappets" hung down. The brow was decorated with a cobra and a vulture.

1327 BCE	c.1320 BCE	c.1120 BCE	1917–1921 CE
Tutankhamen dies, leaving no heir. His widow Ankhesenamun seeks a new husband unsuccessfully	Horemheb, last 18th-dynasty king, completes the return to traditional religion and art	In the crowded Valley of the Kings, Rameses IV's burial site covers Tutankhamen's tomb	Howard Carter successfully searches the Valley of the Kings for Tutankhamen's tomb

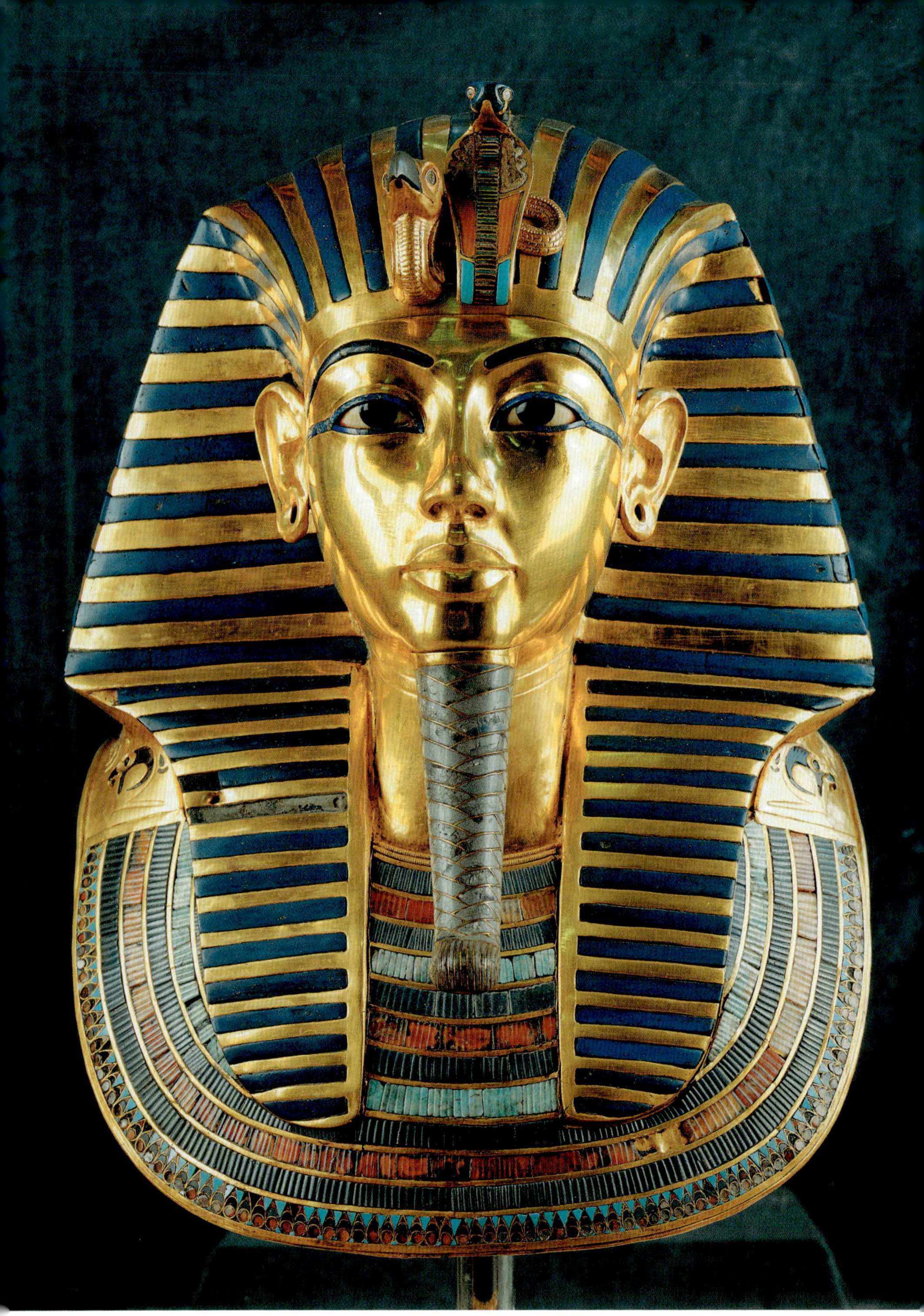

The mask is made of beaten and burnished gold and encrusted with semiprecious stones and colored glass. Tutankhamen also wears a ceremonial plaited beard. Despite the unpopularity of facial hair during life, beards were considered to be a quality of the gods and were thought to be the color of lapis lazuli. On certain occasions, pharaohs would show themselves to be living gods by wearing a false beard secured by a cord. After death, pharaohs were often shown wearing the divine Osirid form of beard, long and plaited with the end jutting forward, as seen here. The rearing cobra on the nemes headdress is known as a "uraeus," which derives from the Greek word for this cobra.

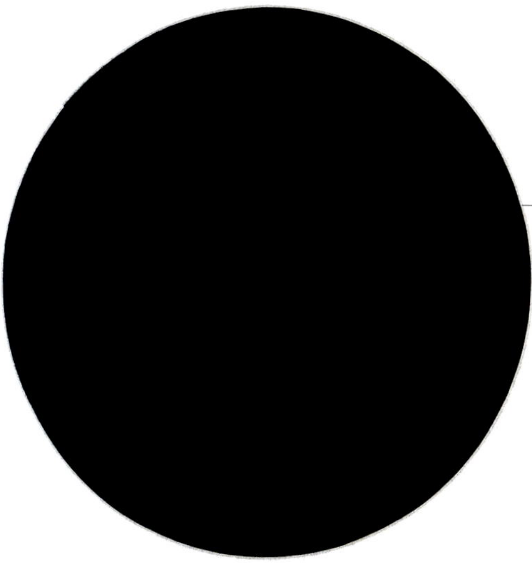

The vulture head and the cobra, with its looped body, are the usual representations, symbolizing the goddesses of Upper and Lower Egypt who protect the king.

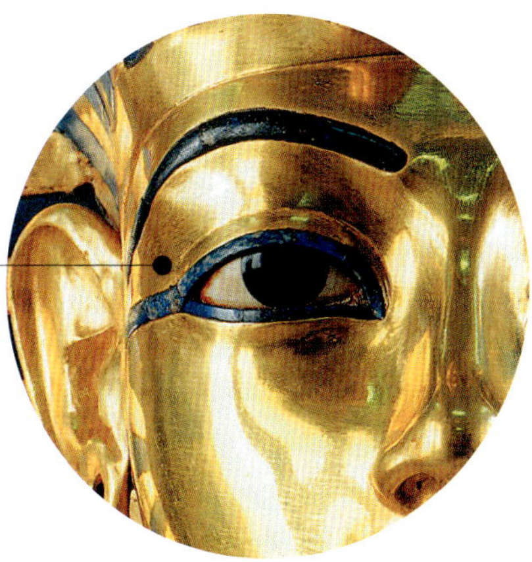

The features are balanced and symmetrical. The eyebrows and lid lines are made of blue glass. The eyes themselves are made of obsidian and quartz.

Predominantly dazzling gold and brilliant blue, this mask was made to inspire reverence in the next world, while the portrayal of the king's facial features was intended to help his soul to recognize him and return to his mummified body in the afterlife. On a flawless gold base, blue glass the color of lapis lazuli denotes the eyebrows and eyeliner. Blue glass was also used to create the headdress stripes and the false beard. The broad collar comprises blue glass, turquoise, carnelian, amazonite quartz, and green feldspar with a lotus-bud border of colored glass cloisonné. In Egyptian mythology the lotus flower was a symbol of the sun, creation, and rebirth. Both men and women wore broad decorative and protective collars—especially the funerary collar, known as the *wesekh*, which has specific theological links to the traditional nine gods and to creation.

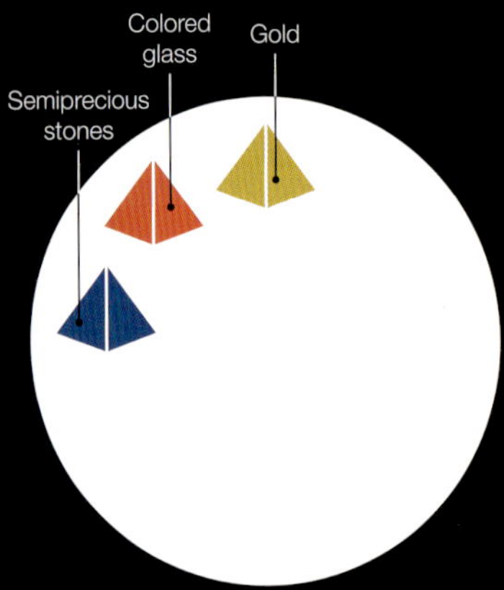

At each end of the collar, the golden falcons' heads are encrusted with obsidian and colored glass, symbolizing Horus, the god of the sky.

The almond-shaped eyes are inlaid with white quartz with pupils of black obsidian. The corners of the eyes are tinted with red pigment and rimmed with bright blue glass to represent the kohl the young king wore in life.

Embedded with colors and shapes associated with everything heavenly, the strong contrasts of blue and gold, and horizontals and verticals, were all designed purposely as charms for eternal life.

The Egyptians called gold "the flesh of the gods" which was appropriate because pharaohs were called gods on earth. This represents some of the highest artistic and technical achievements of the New Kingdom and, since every craftsman's lifestyle and social standing depended on the quality of his skills and experience, it can be assumed that these artisans lived well. Most of the mask was made out of gold sheets joined together by heating and hammering and the embellishments of semiprecious stones and glass were added using the most advanced techniques. Every aspect of the mask, from the smooth surface of the face to the symbolic decorations, the collar, and headdress, is proficiently formed and, more importantly, consistent with accepted beliefs.

The sun god, Ra, traditionally had a body of gold and hair of lapis lazuli—these materials were reflected in the pharaoh's mask.

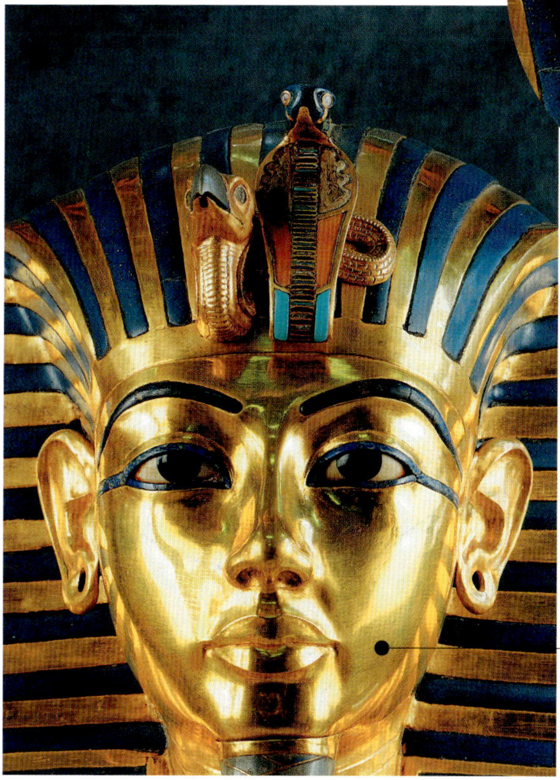

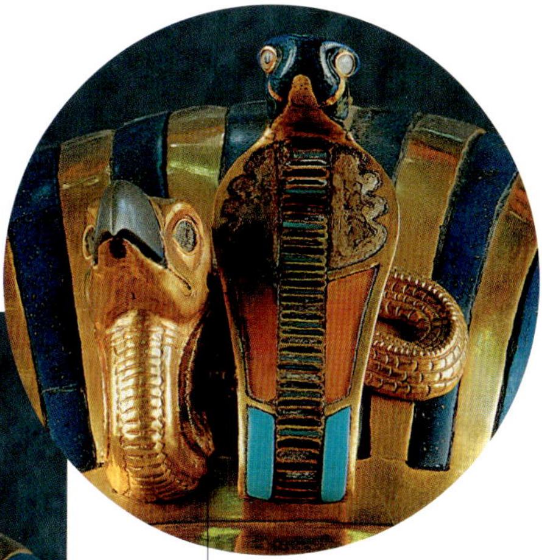

The cobra is gold and dark-blue faience (glazed earthenware), with gold and quartz eyes, and a hood made from carnelian, turquoise glass, and quartz.

The mask was made from two sheets of gold heated over a ceramic furnace until they were malleable and welded together smoothly.

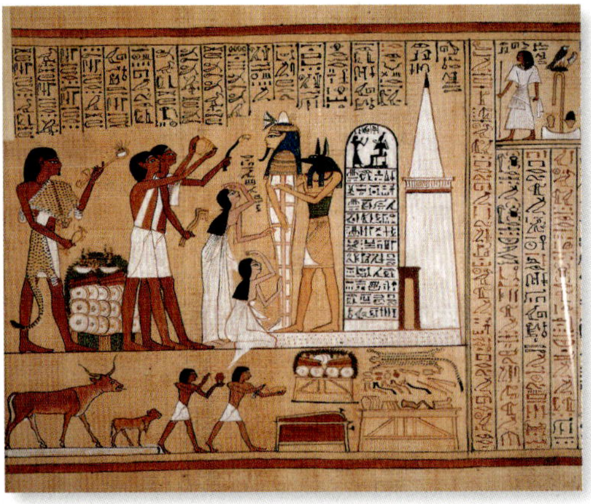

ORIGINALLY FROM THE TOMB OF HUNEFER, THEBES, NOW IN THE BRITISH MUSEUM, LONDON

The Papyrus of Hunefer from the Book of the Dead

Pigment on papyrus, c.1285 BCE

THE OPTIONS FOR BUYING A BOOK OF THE DEAD so that the spells could help the wealthy to pass through to the afterlife after death were varied. Individual bespoke versions could be commissioned or a stock copy could be bought so that scribes could add the name of the buyer in the appropriate places. Interestingly, although training to be a scribe and grasping the complexities of hieroglyphic writing was arduous, once the skills were mastered, scribes became their own bosses and it was considered one of the most distinguished professions.

Hunefer was a nobleman and so in a position to be able to commission his own papyrus. He was wealthy and respected enough to select the amount and

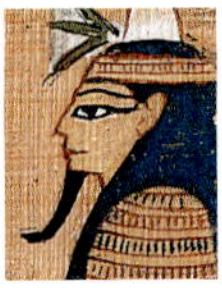

1327–1323 BCE

Reign of Ay, believed to be uncle or great-uncle of Tutankhamun

1323-1295

Reign of Horemheb, whose rule represents a return to comparative normality after the Amarna period

1295

The death of Horemheb sees the end of the 18th dynasty. Rameses I is the first king of the 19th dynasty

choice of chapters, the number and quality of illustrations, and the length of the entire papyrus. In general, scrolls ranged from 15–90 feet by 12–18 inches/4.5–27.5 m by 30–46 cm. It was believed that the deceased took an entire night to travel through the realms of the dead. Using the collection of spells and hymns from their Book of the Dead, they would hopefully pass all the tests and trials unscathed and as the sun rose the next day, they would emerge in the afterlife ready to join the company of the gods. Resplendent with color and information, this section of Hunefer's Book of the Dead shows the Opening of the Mouth ceremony that was performed just after a person had died in the belief that it would revive the body once it reached the afterlife. If the dead were revitalized, they could live in the afterlife and also watch over those still living. This ceremony was performed on statues as well as on mummies and it was believed that once performed, the mummy or statue would be able to eat, breathe, see, hear, and enjoy the offerings and provisions left for them—that their life force, or ka, would flow freely again. The ritual was either carried out by a priest or by the son of the deceased as a final act of piety. Sometimes it was a way of legitimizing the royal succession.

Fact

The special bladed knife might be the same knife used to cut the umbilical cord, while the adze (as seen in Hunefer's papyrus) is a sculptor's tool, so refers to the making and creating of things.

17½ in (45.7 cm)

32½ in (83.4 cm)

1295–1294 BCE

The aging Rameses I reigns for barely one year

1294–1279 BCE

Sety I restores traditional temples and recarves representations of Amun

c.1292 BCE

Sety I reopens several old quarries to begin an extensive building programme

c.1285 BCE

Hunefer dies and, as was customary, his papyrus scroll is buried with him

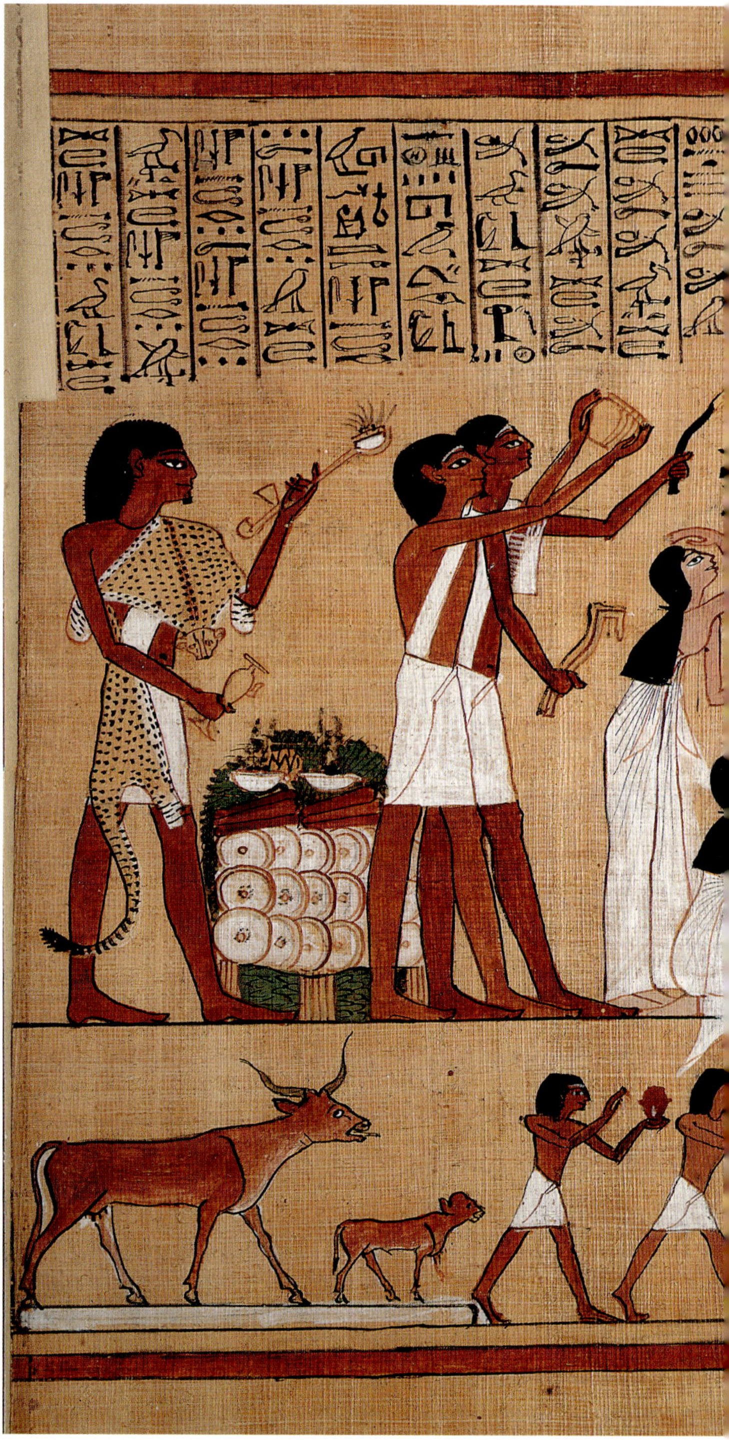

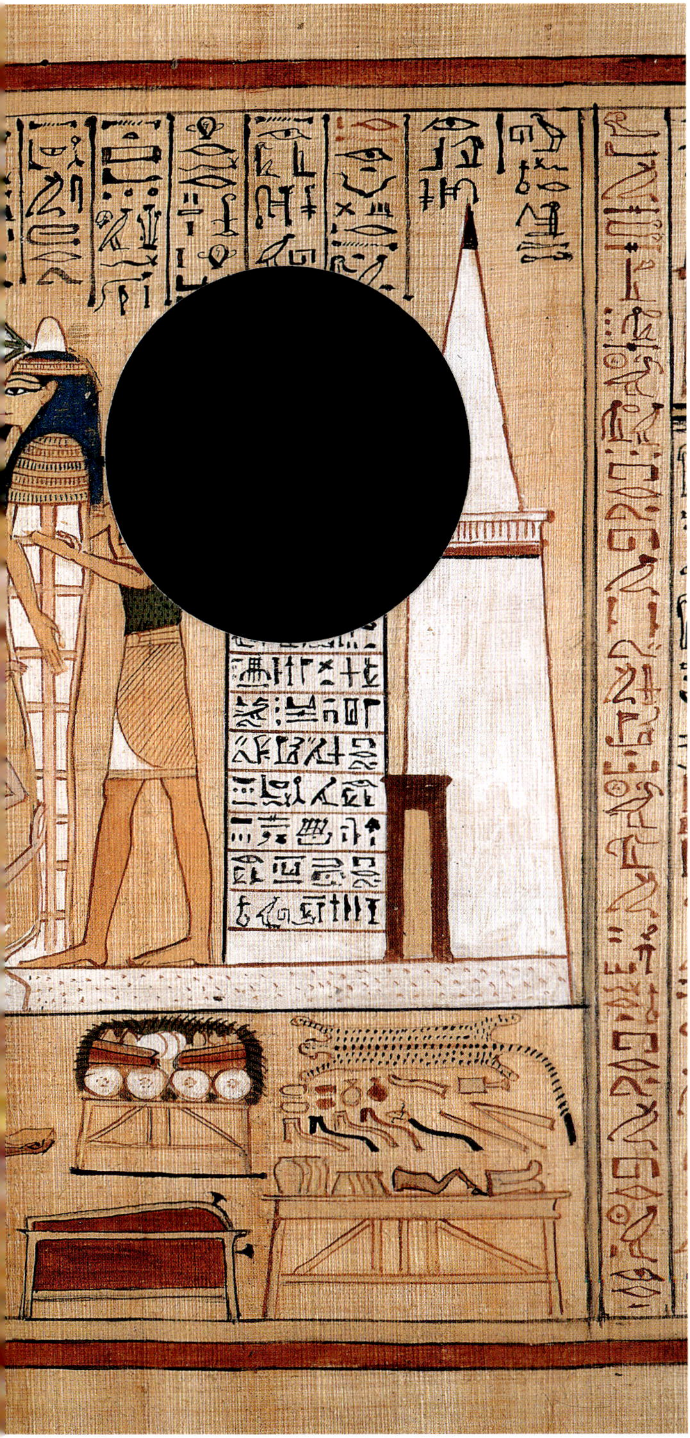

The centerpiece of the upper scene depicts the mummy of Hunefer, supported by either a priest wearing a jackal mask or the god Anubis. Two priests with white sashes are carrying out the Opening of the Mouth ritual. One is holding special implements and the other offers some liquid from a jar. There are four jars in that priest's hand, implying that he pours the liquid four times. Behind them stands the priest in charge wearing a leopard skin and offering incense and a libation (the pouring of a liquid offering as a religious ritual). The two women in front of the mummy are Hunefer's mourning wife and daughter. The white building at the right represents Hunefer's tomb, complete with portal doorway and small pyramid, which were both featured in real tombs of this date in Thebes. At the right of the lower scene is a table bearing the various implements needed for the Opening of the Mouth ritual.

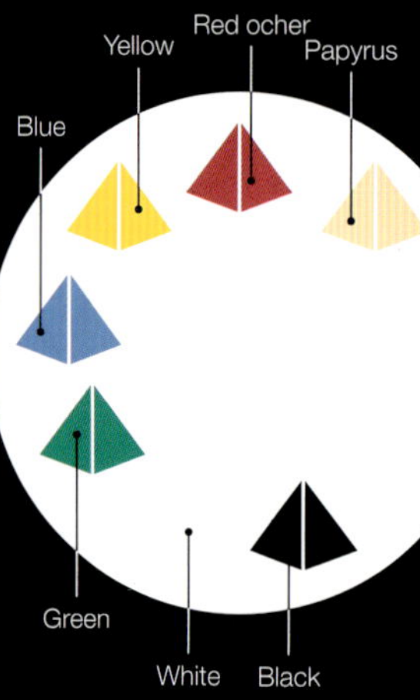

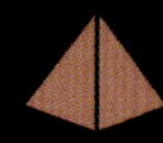

Most of the paints derived from earth minerals or plants; the black came from carbon, white from chalk, and red from ocher and lead.

Although the artist has not specifically shown tone, the two priests performing the rite are distinguished by different shades of brown paint.

The creativity of Egyptian artists lay in producing a new and pleasing combination of the elements to which they had to adhere. Colors, however, could rarely be interfered with. They were expressive rather than natural: men usually had red skin because they were often outside in the sun, and women, children, or middle-aged men were frequently painted with yellow skin. Sometimes—as here—pink skin signified aristocratic women. Blue and gold expressed divinity and the use of black for royal figures indicated the fertility of the Nile from which Egypt was born. Stereotypes were employed to show the geographical origins of foreigners. Colors were blocked-in in flat, opaque washes and fine outlines were either in dark red, brown, or black.

Although the artist was restricted by conventions, he has also managed to experiment. His use of color is subtle and has been used to clarify the story. It draws attention to specific areas of importance and the vividness of the scene.

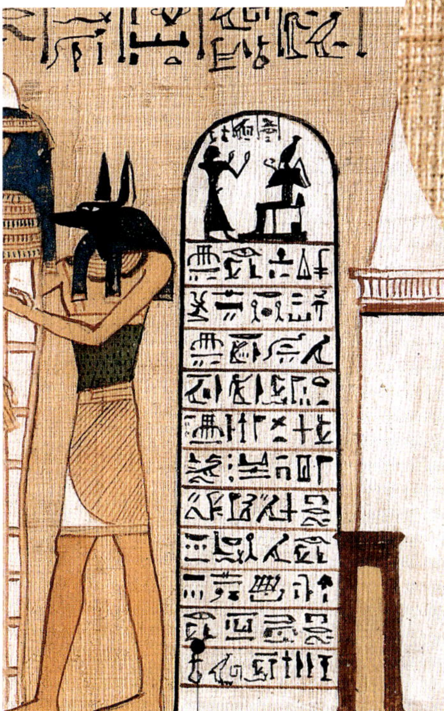

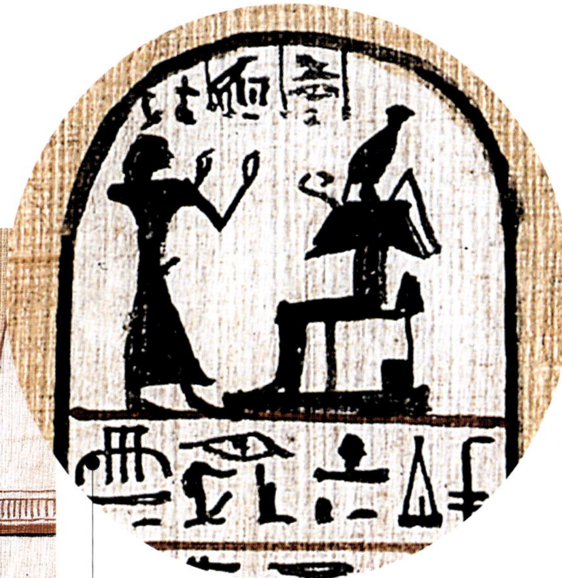

The text is "retrograde"—or written backward—contrary to normal practice, perhaps because it discusses issues of the afterlife.

Water was mixed with the pigment to produce fine liquid suitable for drawing the hieroglyphs. Sometimes milk was added to pigment for the vignettes. Brushes were made from rush stems that had been cut at angles and chewed into fibers.

The hieroglyphs are written in black ink with headings and important passages in red. Pens were made from softened ends of reeds.

During the New Kingdom, the Book of the Dead was not standardized and varied in content and style. Some things were fixed, such as Anubis always being shown as a jackal. Vignettes were considered more specialized to execute so usually take up more space than the hieroglyphs, which are usually fitted in around the images. As long as they conformed to the rules and showed the ceremony clearly, artists could create personal responses. Here, the drooping fold of cloth from Hunefer's daughter's dress hangs over one section of the image and there is an attempt at showing depth as the two main priests overlap. To make sure the content was legible, the large stela of Hunefer worshiping Osiris had to be drawn larger than it really was.

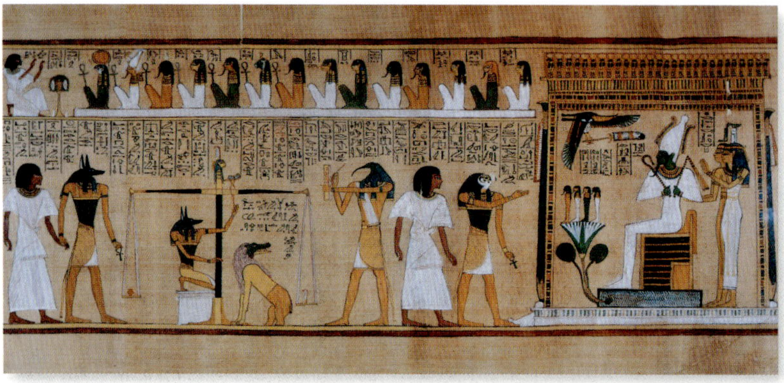

ORIGINALLY FROM THE TOMB OF HUNEFER, THEBES, NOW IN THE BRITISH MUSEUM, LONDON

The Judgment of Hunefer from the Book of the Dead

Ink and pigment on papyrus, c.1285 BCE

THE HIGH OFFICIAL HUNEFER AND HIS WIFE NESHA lived in Thebes during the New Kingdom around 1300 BCE. As a Royal Scribe and Scribe of Divine Offerings as well as an Overseer of Royal Cattle and steward of King Sety I, Hunefer was both important in his own right and close to the king. His high status is reflected in the quality and individual nature of his Book of the Dead, which he commissioned during his lifetime. The papyrus was found in his tomb, although the tomb's location is no longer known.

Since it is in extremely good condition, this Book of the Dead has helped Egyptologists to piece together valuable information about religious thinking and daily life during the 19th dynasty. This particular story, spell number 125, was

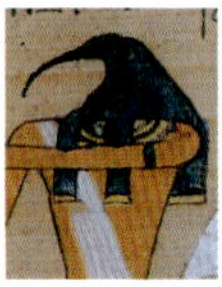

c.1295 BCE

Rameses I completes a new pylon for the temple of Amun-Ra at Karnak

1294 BCE

Wooden "guardian statues" in Rameses I's tomb are influenced by 18th-dynasty art

c.1290 BCE

More resources for new building are taken from Palestine and Syria

extremely important in Egyptian funerary ceremony and the most critical spell in the book. As such, it was always positioned near the beginning of any papyrus.

The Egyptians believed that the heart controlled both the emotions and a person's intelligence. Since the heart was so valued, several spells in the Book of the Dead relate to preventing it from being stolen and making sure of its quick and safe return should that unfortunate event occur. This is the "Weighing of the Heart" ceremony. To find out whether the deceased was worthy enough to continue the journey from Duat (the underworld) to the afterlife, it was believed that the heart was weighed on a set of scales against the "feather of truth." This was a symbolic judgment of a person's character. If the heart was lighter than the feather or if the scales balanced, the person was judged worthy and could proceed on his journey to the next world. If the heart was heavier than the feather, the person was judged to be unworthy and was devoured by the monster Ammit, a strange creature with the head of a crocodile and hindquarters of a hippopotamus. Maat was the goddess of truth and justice and so the Hall of Maat was the hall where the Judgment of the Dead was performed. Here, Anubis (the god who protects the deceased and their tombs) leads Hunefer to the scales of Maat. Anubis weighs Hunefer's heart against the feather of truth while ibis-headed Thoth notes down the correct answers.

Fact

Osiris was the god of the underworld. He was a green-skinned man in the form of a mummified pharaoh. His wife was Isis, and his son was Horus.

$15\frac{1}{2}$ in (39 cm)

c.1287 BCE

Libyan tribes, motivated by famine, try to settle in Egypt

c.1285 BCE

Sety I builds a temple in Abydos in honour of the ancestral kings of the early dynasties

c.1280 BCE

Reliefs on the hypostyle hall are in a new, more realistic style

1279 BCE

Paintings in Sety I's tomb are among the most elegant of the New Kingdom

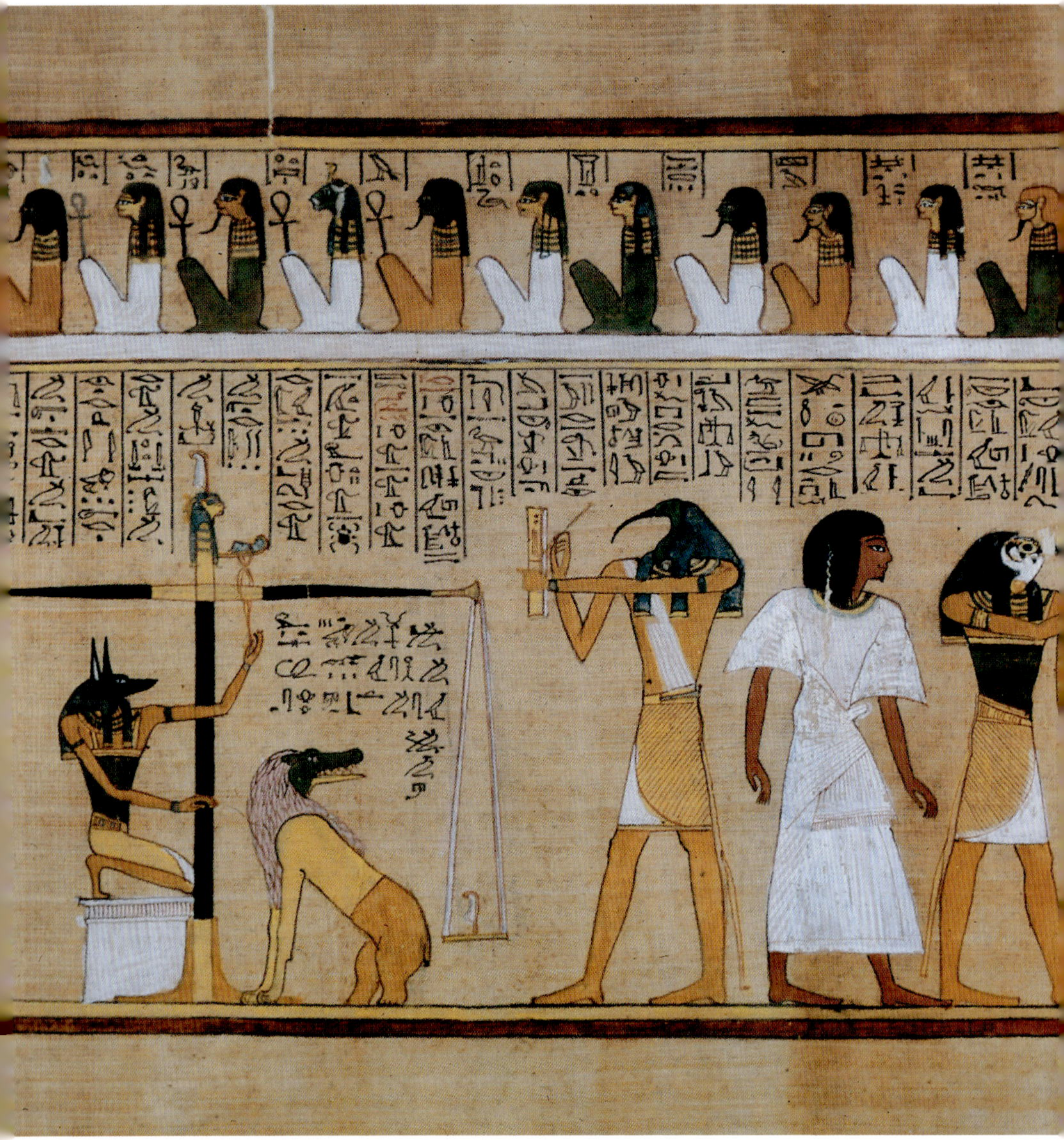

Full of symbolism, this papyrus is conventionally planned but imaginatively executed. Across the top, 14 gods and goddesses sit and assess Hunefer. They present him with a long list of sins and he has to deny each in turn. Each time he does, the feather is weighed against his heart to test the reliability of his denials. Having passed the test, Hunefer is then led by Horus, the sky god with a falcon's head, to meet Osiris who sits under a canopy on a throne floating on

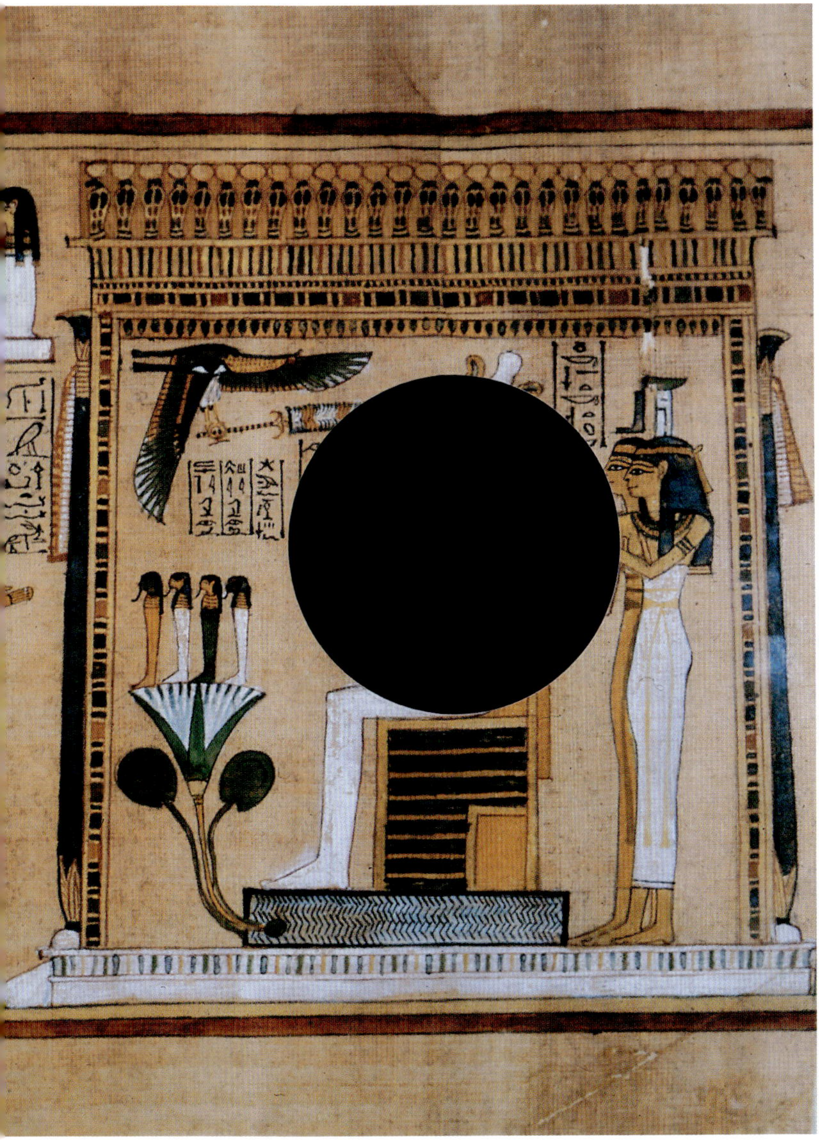

a pool of water, from which a sacred lotus flower emerges. Standing on its petals are the four sons of Horus who were the guardians of the internal organs of the deceased. Each was associated with a particular organ and also with a different cardinal point on the compass; so for instance, Hapi was allied with the lungs and the compass point north. Behind the throne stand two powerful goddesses: Isis and her sister Nephthys.

Egyptian artists used three different types of yellow. Lead antimonate is pale yellow, lead white can darken to slight yellow over time, and orpiment is a relatively strong yellow that fades in direct sunlight. The synthetically prepared lead antimonate is mainly used here.

All the pigments used, except Egyptian blue, made opaque or semi-opaque paints, but Egyptian blue was dark enough to appear opaque.

Flat, opaque paints were considered to be best practice. This artist has not attempted any change in tone or modeling of form, as was customary on these funerary documents.

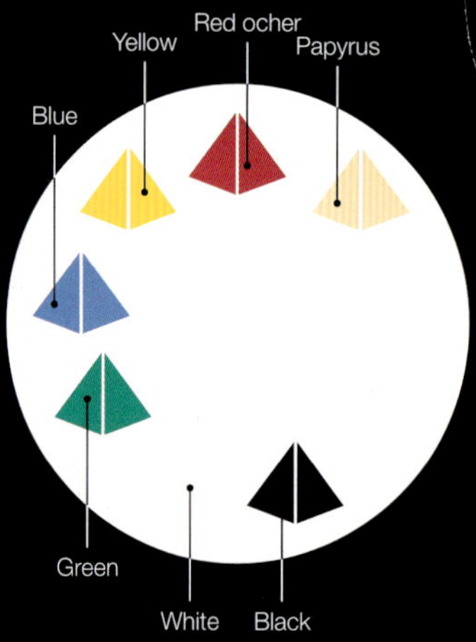

Even though he has adhered to the use of only clear lines and simple shapes, the artist has applied flat areas of color to create a sense of order and balance. Yet the brilliance of the color used helps to bring the story vividly to life and adds to the symbolism. White and blue are used across the image, signifying holiness and purity and giving the image balance. Green was the color of vegetation and new life, and was associated with healing and protective powers—for example, Osiris is green. The skin and parts of the clothing of Anubis, Thoth, Horus, Isis, and Nephthys are yellow signifying gold because of their divinity.

Hieroglyphs are generally read right to left but can also read left to right. The way for us to tell is to read "into" the faces of any animal and human hieroglyphs.

Using the same conventions as all earlier Egyptian art, the style has changed but the artist has adhered to a geometric format.

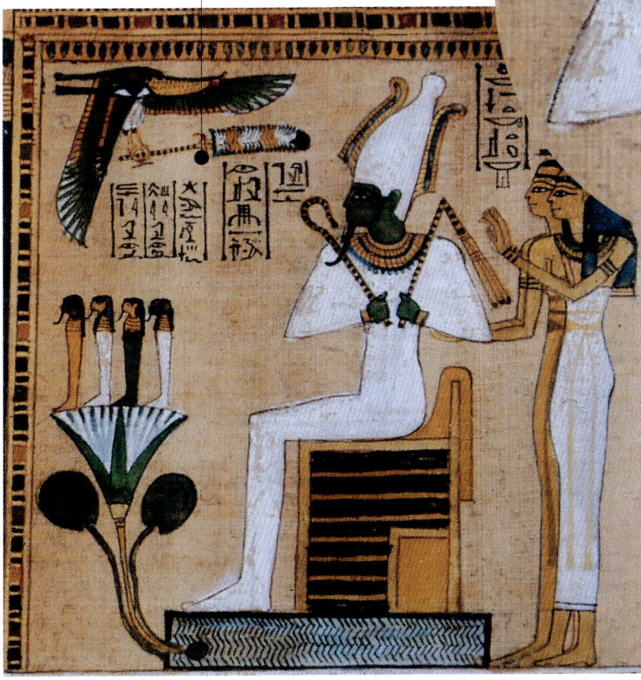

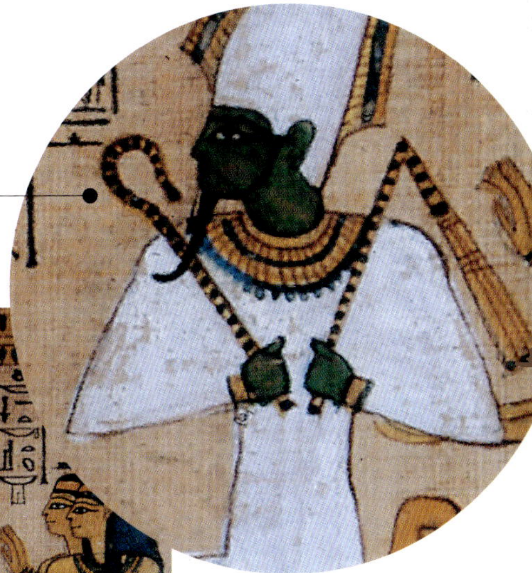

Every aspect is planned and orderly. One red line and one yellow line border the images and the hieroglyphs are fitted around and between the vignettes in vertical columns. The continuous scenes are arranged systematically in monochrome and watercolors of delicacy and brilliance.

Books of the Dead were often preprepared in workshops, with spaces left for the name of the deceased to be written in later. Even custom-made books, like this one, could be the work of several different scribes and artists whose work was literally pasted together. The cost of a typical book could be equivalent to half a year's salary of a laborer, so the purchase was usually planned well in advance of the person's death. This was even more costly. The blank papyrus used for the scroll was usually the most expensive part of the work. The vignettes were so important that artists drew them as large as possible, leaving the scribes to shorten the text to fit the space available under the image.

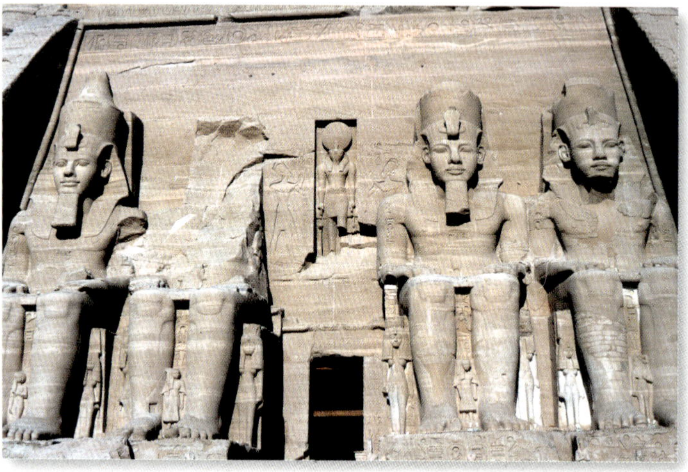

NEAR ASWAN, SOUTHERN EGYPT

The Temple of Rameses II at Abu-Simbel

Sandstone,
c.1284–1264 BCE

The two massive temples carved into the rock cliff face at Abu Simbel were the crowning achievement of Rameses II's reign. They were intended to inspire fear, awe, and reverence among subjects living nearby as a reminder of the pharaoh, because Rameses ruled far away in the north of the country. The larger of the two temples honored Rameses himself, linking him with the gods Amun-Ra, Ra-Horakhty, and Ptah, and the smaller temple honored Queen Nefertari, linking her with the goddess Hathor, who was goddess of many things, including love, destruction, and death. Because Amun-Ra was the sun god and Hathor was his wife, symbolically the two temples bring the royal couple and the gods together as one.

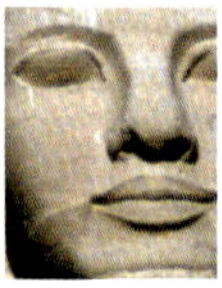

c.1300–1090

Deir el-Medina is occupied by royal workmen and nicknamed "village of the artisans"

1278 BCE

Seti I dies, one year after his son, Rameses II, is crowned

c.1275 BCE

Battle of Kadesh is fought between the Egyptians and the Hittites

The temples were first built as a lasting monument to commemorate Rameses II's alleged victory at the Battle of Kadesh and to intimidate his Nubian neighbors. After 20 years of building, in the twenty-fourth year of his reign, the temples were ready for dedication and it was recorded that Rameses, Nefertari, and their daughter Merytamun sailed up the Nile to reach them. Yet it is likely that Nefertari died suddenly just before the opening celebration because an inscription describing the investiture does not mention her and there are no later records of her alive.

Seven years later an earthquake brought down one of the statues of Rameses and cracked the columns and door of the great hall. Over the centuries, the temples became vulnerable to rising sands. When Greek mercenaries passed by in the 6th century BCE, the sand had reached the knees of the statues—evidence of this is in their carved names on the statues at this height. In 1813 CE, the temples were rediscovered and sand cleared away. In the late 1950s, it became apparent that the rising waters of Lake Nasser (a huge artificial reservoir formed after the building of the Aswan Dam on the River Nile) would engulf the temples completely. After several desperate attempts to save the temples, in the 1960s it was agreed to cut the stone into blocks and to lift them about 200 ft (60 m) above the reservoir on an artificial hill made from a concrete dome. Their reconstruction, in the exact same relationship to each other and the sun as they had been originally, was a magnificent achievement.

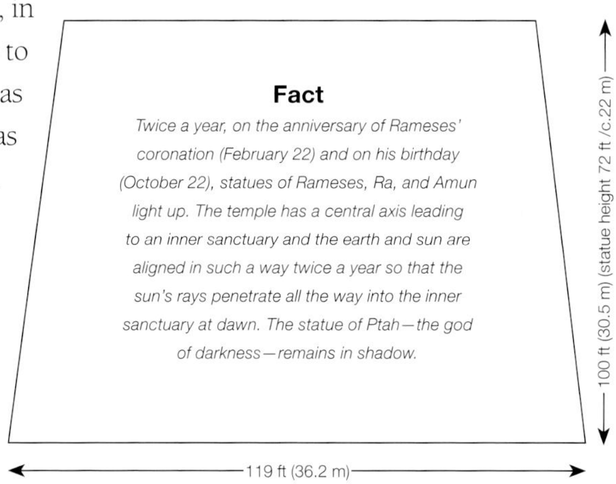

Fact

Twice a year, on the anniversary of Rameses' coronation (February 22) and on his birthday (October 22), statues of Rameses, Ra, and Amun light up. The temple has a central axis leading to an inner sanctuary and the earth and sun are aligned in such a way twice a year so that the sun's rays penetrate all the way into the inner sanctuary at dawn. The statue of Ptah—the god of darkness—remains in shadow.

c.1274 BCE

Earliest known peace treaty is signed following the Battle of Kadesh

1255 BCE

Inauguration of Rameses' two temples takes place in February

c.1250 BCE

Particular type of valuable glass is developed using a technical process involving copper

c.1250 BCE

Rameses II builds fortresses at the Libyan border and fights several wars

The Great Temple—or larger of the two temples—is dedicated to Rameses II. A statue of Rameses II is seated with Amun-Ra, Ra-Horakhty, and Ptah within the innermost part; the sanctuary. The temple's façade is guarded by four colossal statues of the pharaoh, each over 67 ft (20.5 m) high. At the top of the wall behind the statues, a frieze of baboons greets the rising sun. Each statue of Rameses is seated on a throne and wears the double crown of Upper and Lower Egypt. One statue remains demolished from the waist up from the ancient earthquake. The thrones are decorated on their sides with Nile gods symbolically uniting Egypt. Between the legs of the statues and on each of their sides stand smaller statues of members of the royal family. Inside the temple is a great columned hall leading through to the inner sanctuary. The great hall is decorated with records of the king's victories and enemies.

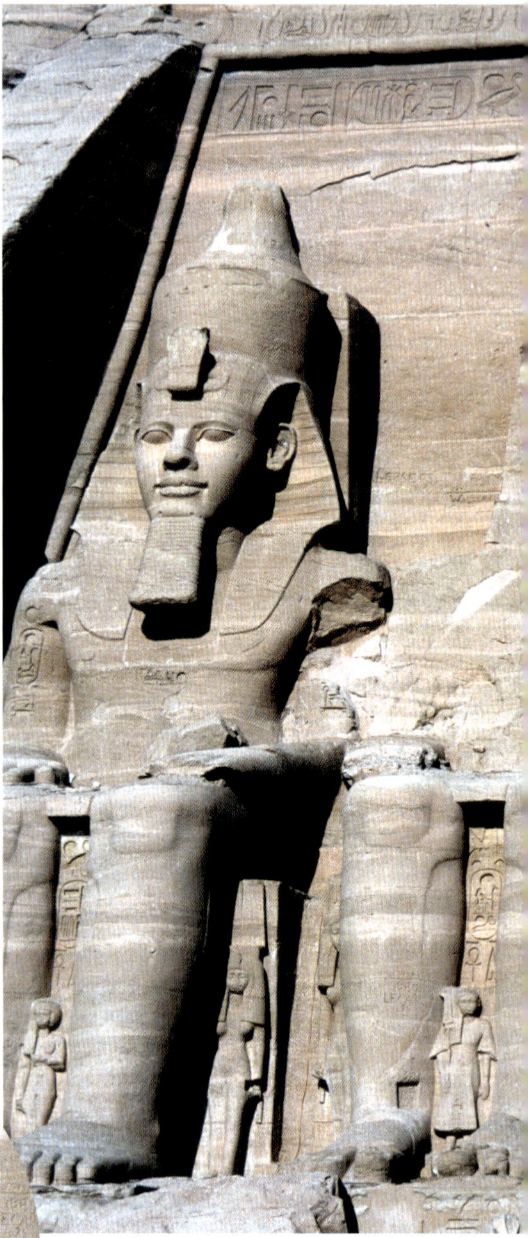

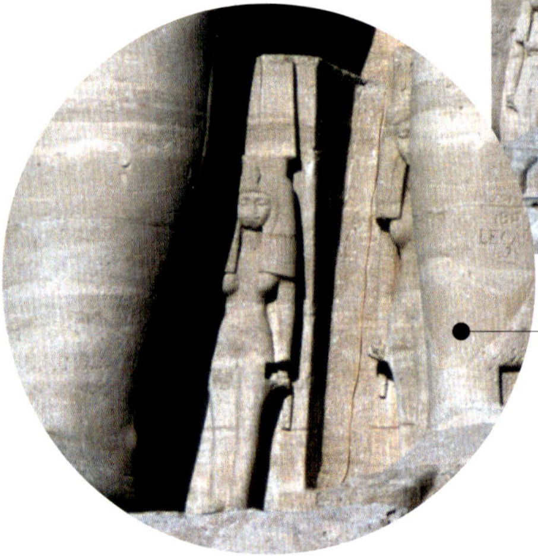

This smaller carving by Rameses' left leg is believed to represent his favorite wife, Nefertari. Although smaller than the main statues, it is carved with just as much attention to detail.

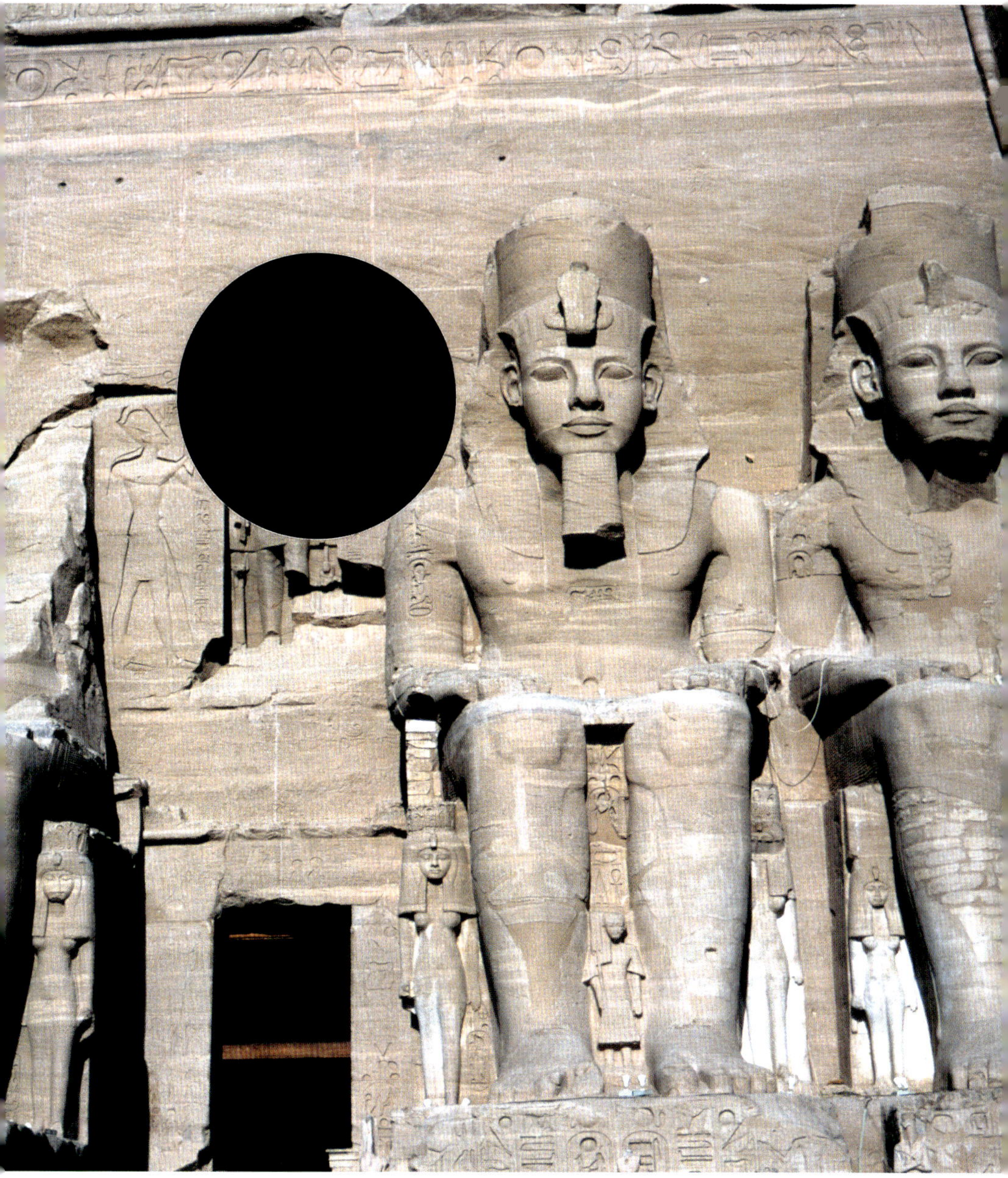

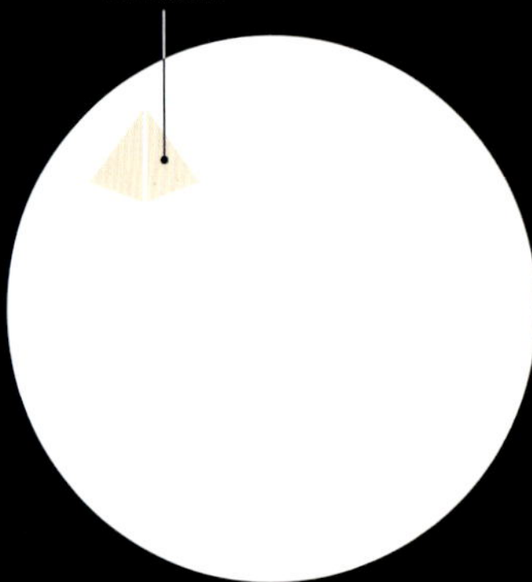

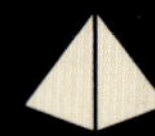

The size and solemn frontal pose of the statues designates them as guardians of the entrances they flank.

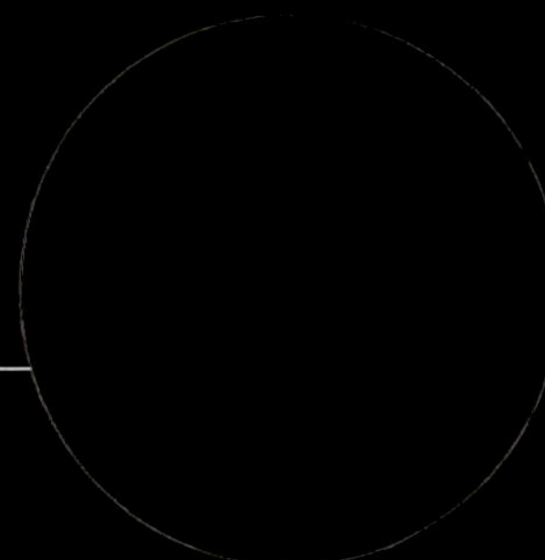

The young, handsome face was finely carved with chisels and grinding stones, then polished with sand.

The smaller statues of relatives carved around the bases of the colossal statues of Rameses were probably, for the first southern colossus: Queen Nefertari by the left leg; the king's mother, the great wife of Sety I, Muttuya by his right leg; and Prince Amenhirkhopshef in front. For the second southern colossus: Princess Bent'anta; Princess Nebettawyby; and one unnamed female figure, probably a lesser royal wife named Esenofre, stand by the legs. The family statues at the first northern colossus were: Queen Nefertari; Princess Beketmut; and Prince Riameses in front. Around the second northern colossus were: Princess Merytamun; Queen Muttuya; and Princess Nofretari; and beneath these sculptures are carved figures of bound captives—all helping to create order out of chaos.

These statues are about 72 ft (22 m) high. Graffiti made by 19th-century visitors half way up the legs proves how deeply they had become buried in the sand.

Rameses wears a double crown and a heavy nemes headdress. The line of the smiling lips is more than a yard (1 m) long. Baboons were depicted because they were thought to help Ra defeat nighttime darkness so were nicknamed *Watchers of the Dawn*.

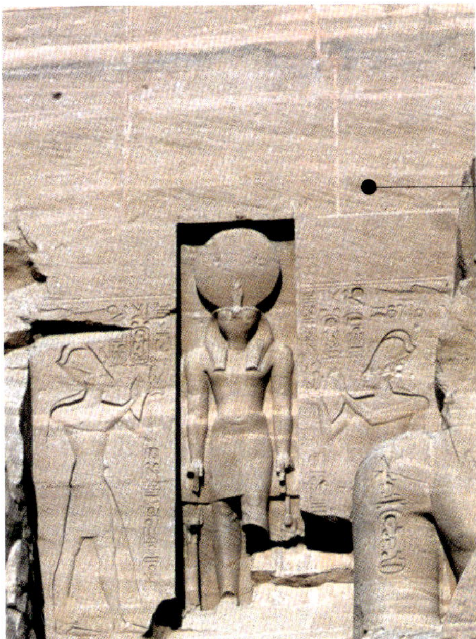

The sandstone slabs were sculpted directly from the rock in which the temple was located. The facade is 108 ft (33 m) high and 125 ft (38 m) broad.

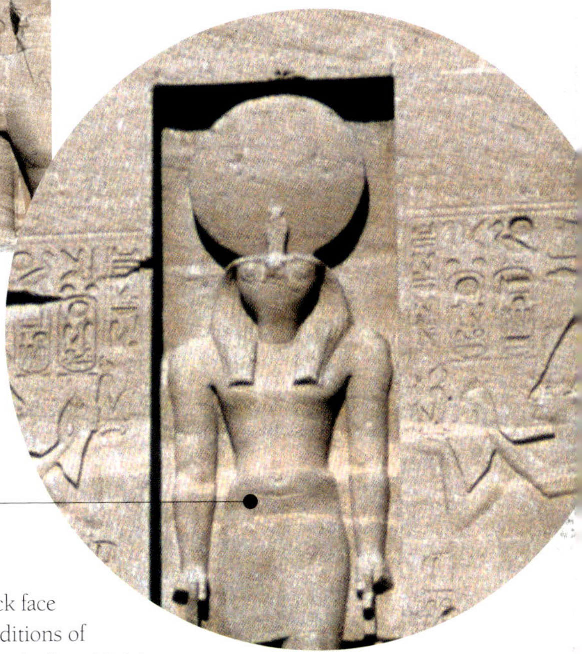

The doorway to the interior is 23 ft (7 m) high. A statue of Ra-Horakhty with a falcon head is in a niche over the entrance, flanked by low reliefs of Rameses presenting him with a statuette of Maat, goddess of truth and justice.

To cut this temple 206 ft (63 m) into the rock face while conforming as much as possible to traditions of temple building was an amazing feat. Builders had to think in three-dimensional reversal—because they were essentially building inside out. Throughout, the highest traditions of craftsmanship have been maintained and artists demonstrated remarkable flexibility with the rules of art when necessary.

For instance, because the colossi were carved from the same rock as the temples, there was no space on the façade for images of the king suppressing the forces of chaos, traditionally shown on the outside of temples. Instead, this is addressed in the great hall with delicate raised reliefs of battles and victories.

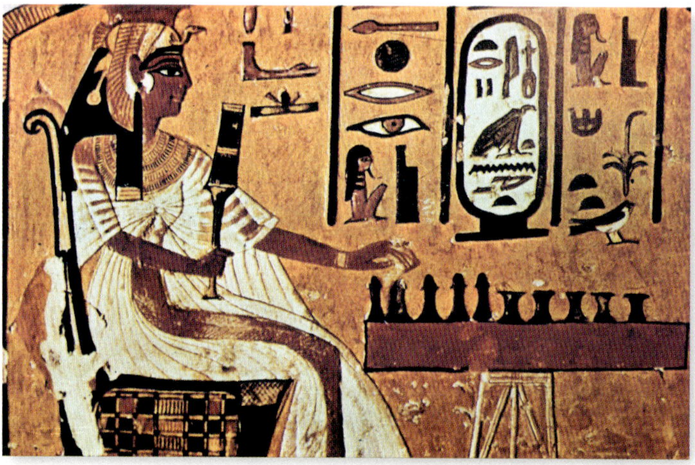

VALLEY OF THE QUEENS, THEBES

Wall Painting in the Tomb of Queen Nefertari

Fresco on raised relief,
1255 BCE

During the 19th dynasty, decorated tombs for important royal women and children began to be built to the south of the Valley of the Kings at Thebes. The area is now called the Valley of the Queens. As a reflection of their high status, these tombs were built by royal workmen and decorated by royal artists and craftsmen. The most famous of these was commissioned by Rameses II for his favorite wife, Nefertari. Her tomb has been called one of the most beautiful in Egypt, appropriately perhaps for the queen who was known as "the most beautiful of them." For about 25 years of Rameses II's long reign, Nefertari enjoyed great influence and prestige. Rameses had both a small temple built for her and her painted tomb. Like Nefertiti, her name begins with "nefer"

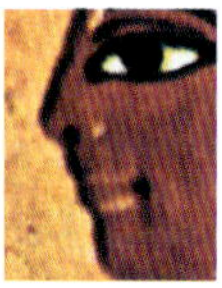

c.1295–1255 BCE

As Rameses II's much-loved wife, it is believed that Nefertari died in the 25th year of her husband's reign

c.1286–1265 BCE

King Hattusilus III rules the Hittite people in a country directly north of Egypt

1279–1213 BCE

Often described as Egypt's most powerful pharaoh, Rameses II rules for 67 years

meaning beautiful and, as is clear from their art, the ancient Egyptians valued beauty highly. Like Nefertiti, images of her often show her the same size as her husband, when usual practice was to make wives smaller.

Unearthed in 1904 by an Italian expedition, the tomb began to deteriorate badly through damp, the effects of visitors' breath, and salt crystallization behind the plaster on which the artists had applied the paint. Fear of further damage resulted in the closing of the tomb in 1934. Many attempts at conservation were made and in 1988 an international team of experts began implementing various methods of stabilization. The plaster was strengthened and damaged areas were carefully repaired and cleaned. Restored to its former glory, in 1995 it was reopened to the public.

In this particular wall painting, one of many different images of Nefertari featured in the tomb, she is playing Senet, a chesslike board game that had strong religious connotations. The board consisted of 30 squares in 3 rows of 10 and movement of the playing pieces was determined by tossing knucklebones or sticks with different colored sides. Possibly the oldest board game in the world, Senet was believed to have the ability to help the deceased negotiate the dangerous journey to the afterlife. It was also featured in several other tomb paintings from the Old and Middle Kingdoms. By the New Kingdom, it had become even more important. If a (deceased) player was lucky, he or she would be protected by the gods Ra, Thoth, and sometimes Osiris.

Fact

Rameses II confirmed his love for Nefertari when he dedicated a small temple at Abu Simbel in Nubia to both her and the goddess Hathor, so bestowing upon his wife the status of a goddess.

c.5½ ft (1.6 m)

6 ft (1.8 m)

1279

Rameses II assumes the throne. Over his reign, he celebrates 14 "Sed" festivals (which celebrate the continued rule of a pharaoh)

1260 BCE

According to Homer, the fall of Troy occurs in this year

1260 BCE

Possibly the year of Egypt's 10 plagues and therefore the Israelites' exodus

1255 BCE

Prince Mery-Atum, the 16th child of Rameses and Nefertari, born in the year Nefertari dies

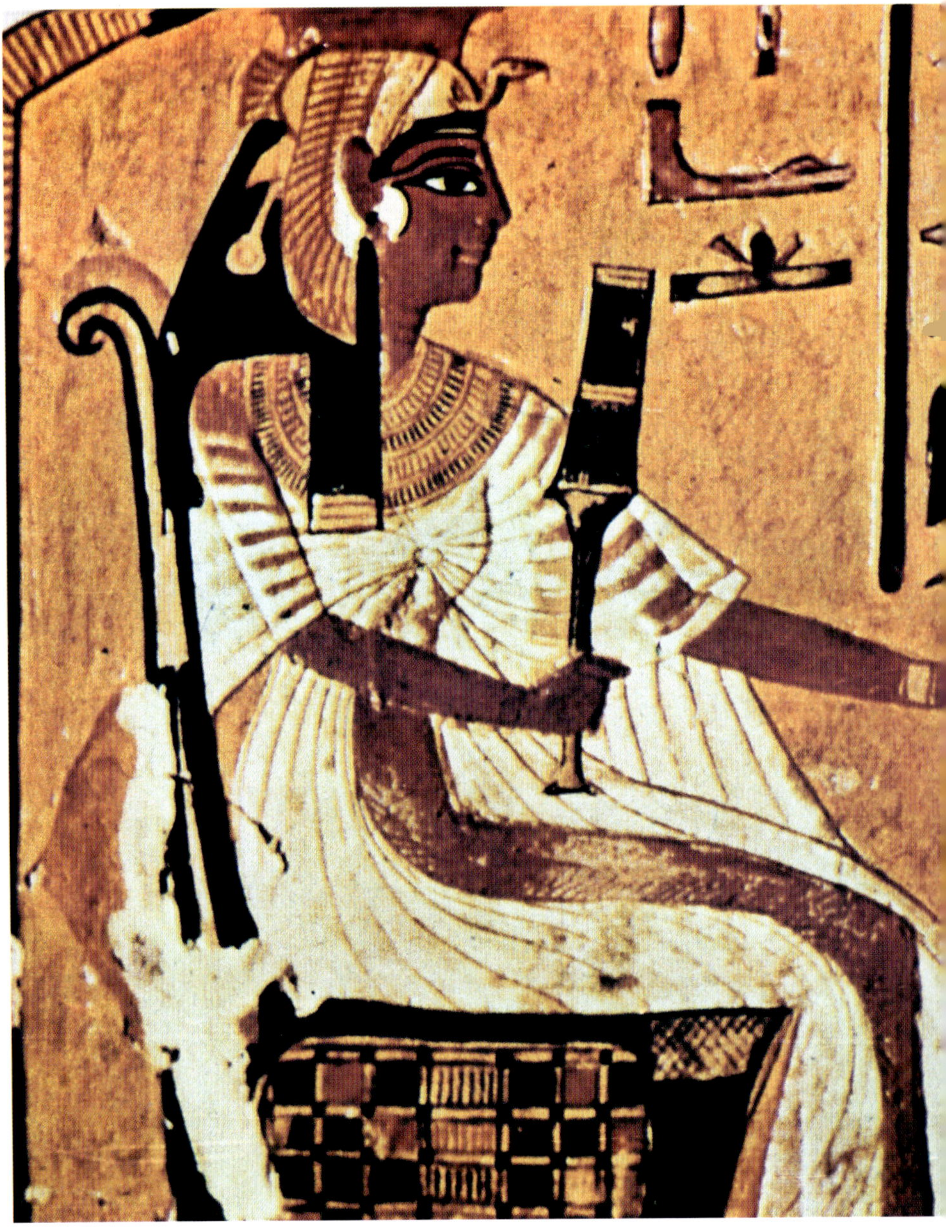

Nefertari had many official titles: "Great Royal Wife," "Lady of Two Lands," "Mistress of Upper and Lower Egypt," and even "God's Wife." She was also known as: "Lady of Charm," "Sweet of Love," and "Rich of Praise." These names imply that she was kind as well as beautiful, and she was possibly the only Egyptian queen honored with such a magnificent burial place. On its walls and corridors, some 5,600 square feet (520 m^2) of wall paintings illustrate her journey to the next world. The Senet board had 30 squares with

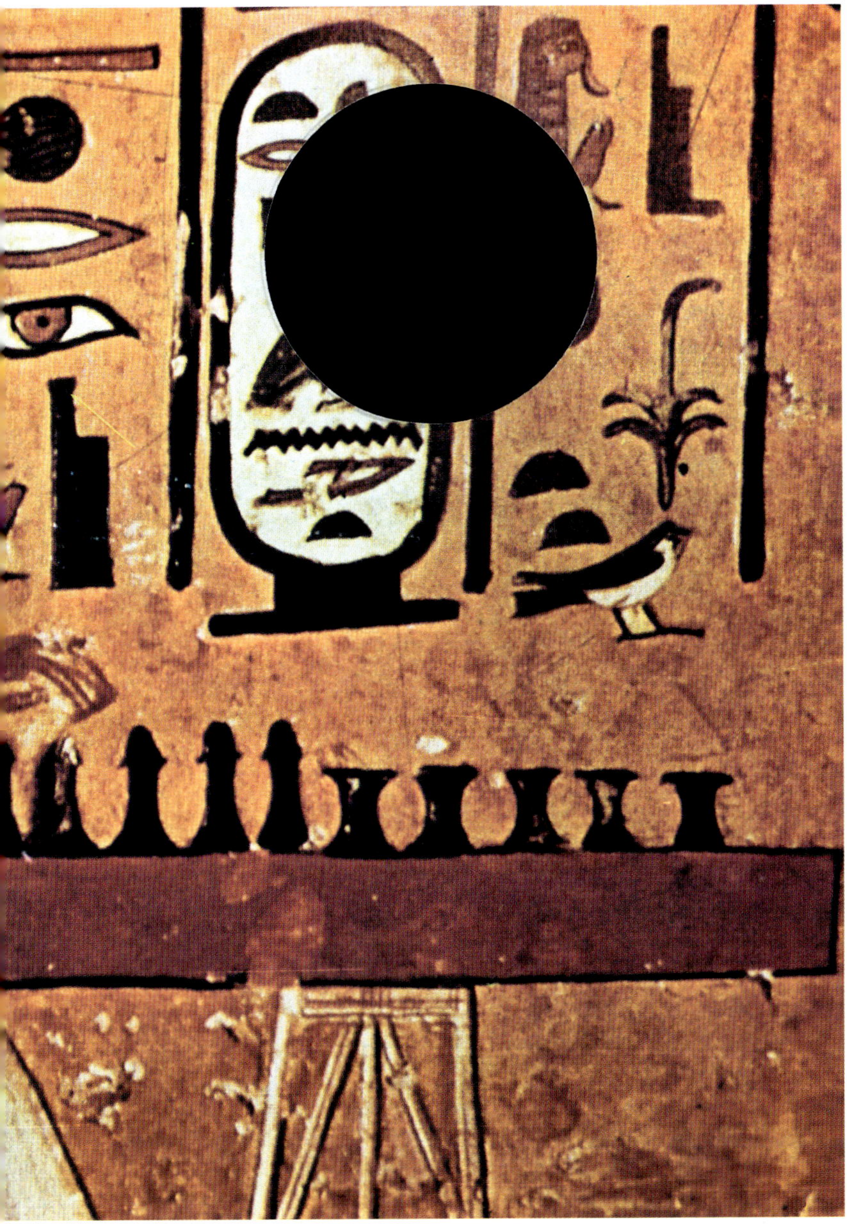

movable gaming pieces called "the dancers." Nefertari is represented playing the game alone, as her unseen opponent symbolizes Fate who must be defeated in order to gain immortality in the afterlife. This image is situated in the first chamber of Nefertari's tomb and comes directly from the Book of the Dead. Sitting on a high-backed chair, resting on a reed mat, the queen, dressed in a white gown, is framed within a shelter made of reeds.

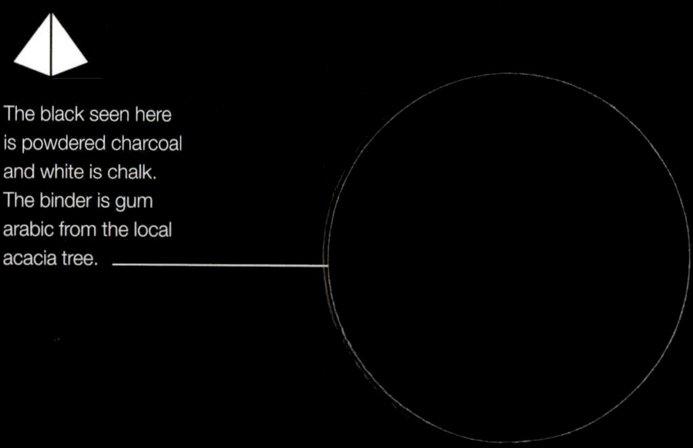

Earth colors (reds and yellows) were made from burned umber, or cooked iron oxide. Some reds came from trace amounts of manganese while yellow came from hydrated iron oxide or ocher. Blues and greens were compounded from natural copper ores: malachite or azurite. Some of these ores were cooked with calcium and quartz or other forms of silica, producing a glasslike substance that was then pulverized.

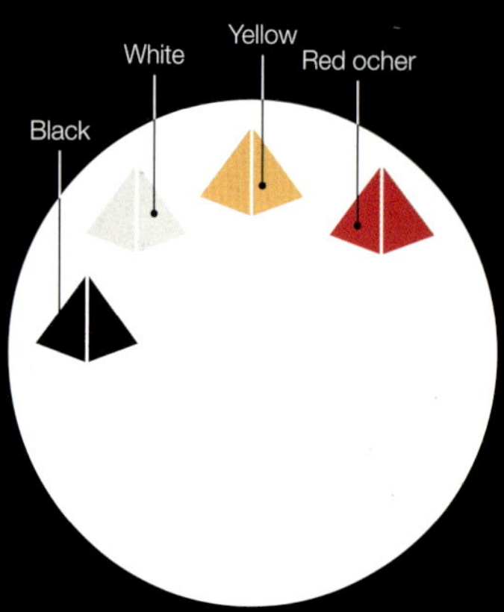

Once the walls had been primed with plaster, they were painted in brilliant colors. The multitude of hues used was exceptional for the time, with variations of colors set against strong blacks and blue-whites. Paints used consisted of pigment, water to make the paint flow, and gum to bind it to the surface of the wall. The palette was limited to vivid, primary colors with few nuances between shades. Most of the pigments were mineral, not organic, and some were applied quite thickly, in an *impasto* style. Wearing white sandals and a vulture headdress, Nefertari holds a scepter in her right hand and is about to move a Senet piece with her left. The rest of the space is filled with Nefertari's name and titles.

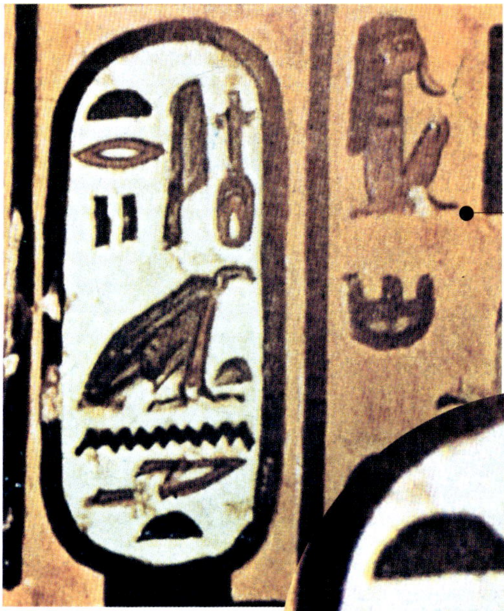

The low relief technique used here was common on tomb walls at this time and patterns reflect contemporary textile patterns.

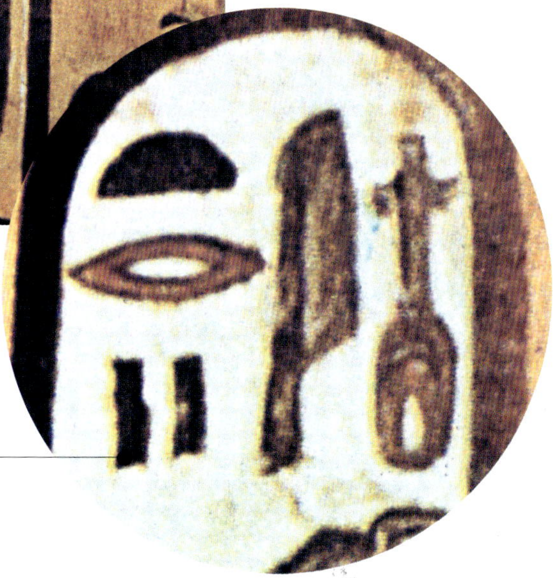

The low relief technique creates shadows, giving the image dynamism and a sense of three-dimensional volume.

The surface of this painting is coated with tree resin and egg white. Used chiefly as a glaze on the red and yellow areas, the coating enhances the brilliance of the color beneath, which in turn emphasizes the action of the image. The limestone in the Valley of the Queens was not of the best quality and so was not well suited to painting or carving. Several layers of thick plaster had to be applied to the whole tomb, walls and ceiling, to create a suitable surface for the paintings. Vignettes and texts were lightly carved in raised relief into the dry plaster and then the walls were primed with a gypsum wash before the artists painted the images on the top.

The tomb is decorated in brightly painted relief, which, owing to the poor condition of the limestone in the Valley of the Queens, was cut into layers of plaster applied on top of the stone.
It is believed that the painters used a glaze over the paint, probably beeswax, tree resin, or egg white, which may account for the brilliance of the colors.

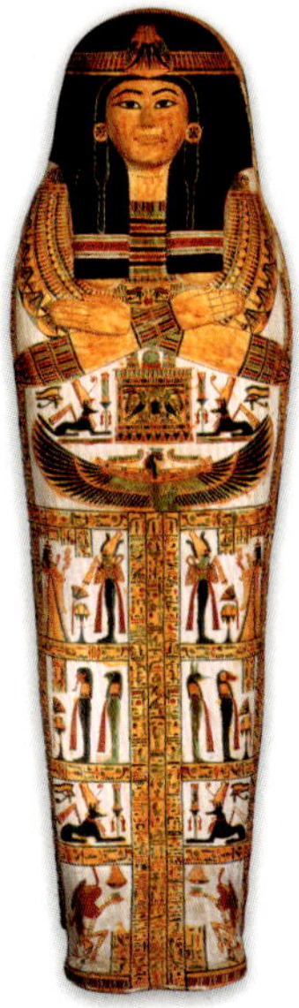

FROM DEIR EL-BAHRI, WESTERN THEBES, NOW IN THE METROPOLITAN MUSEUM OF ART, NEW YORK

Outer Coffin of Henettawy

Gessoed and painted wood, 1040–991 BCE

HENETTAWY LIVED DURING THE REIGN of Pharaoh Psusennes I, of the 21st dynasty during the Third Intermediate Period, which directly followed the New Kingdom. During most of this period, the ruling power was divided between the royal dynasty based in the city of Tanis in the Nile Delta, and the high priests of Amun at Thebes, who had their own "dynasty" during this time. By this time, kingship had lost its prestige and pharaohs no longer built grand mortuary temples or tombs in the Valley of the Kings. During this unsettled

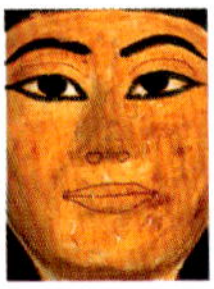

1070–1044 BCE

Smendes founds the 21st dynasty and ends the New Kingdom

1070–712 BCE

Third Intermediate Period is characterized by political instability

1069 BCE

Rameses XI dies and Egypt gradually loses influence and control period, individual private tombs were abandoned in favor of family tombs, built into the rocks, which could be more easily guarded from thieves.

Fundamental changes in burial customs meant that decorated tomb chapels were no longer part of the rituals, and inside the plain rock-cut burial chambers there were no paintings or reliefs. Scenes that were once painted or carved on tomb walls were now painted onto wooden coffins instead and onto papyri that were placed inside the coffins. Such was the loss of grandeur, that tombs were even reused if they had previously been robbed.

Henettawy (who was buried in a reused tomb) was described as "a mistress of the house and chantress of Amun-Ra." In other words, she was a priestess and singer in the Temple of Amun at Thebes. She was also the granddaughter of a queen and her father was the High Priest Menkheperre, who effectively ruled the south of the country during his lifetime. As a result, Henettawy was an important figure in society, so she could afford two coffins—one inner and one outer—and higher quality paintings on both. Since her tomb was undecorated, in accordance with the fashions of the time, the paintings on her coffin, with their emphasis on elaborate religious symbolism and imagery, were intricate and detailed. When she died during her twenties, the art of coffin decoration was at its height. It reflects a style and iconography that had developed during the late New Kingdom and developed even more during the 21st dynasty, when funerary beliefs began emphasizing the merging of the gods Ra-Horakhty with Osiris. This, along with other subtle changes, meant that artists had greater scope (not necessarily freedom) than during earlier periods.

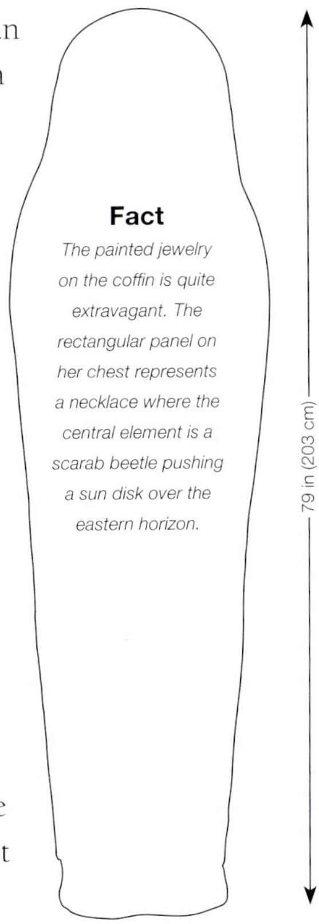

Fact

The painted jewelry on the coffin is quite extravagant. The rectangular panel on her chest represents a necklace where the central element is a scarab beetle pushing a sun disk over the eastern horizon.

c.1051 BCE

Approximate date of the Biblical King Saul of Israel

1044 BCE

Smendes, the first king of the 21st dynasty, dies

1044–1040 BCE

Amenemnisu succeeds Smendes, but Henettawy's father Menkheperre controls the country

1040–992 BCE

Psusennes I rules Egypt, the third king of the 21st dynasty

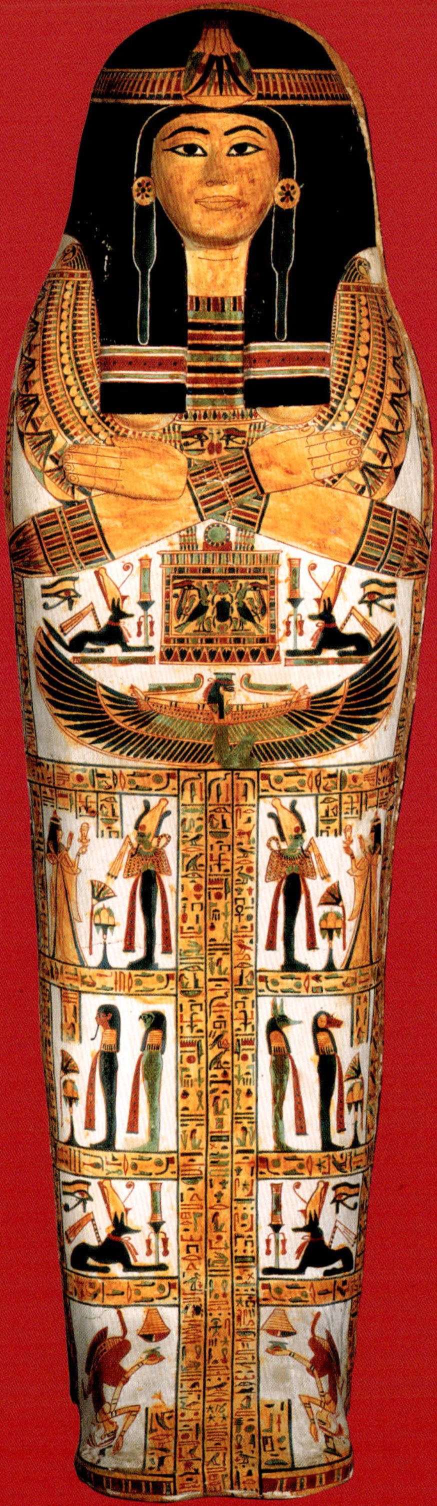

Compared to the somewhat plain jewelry she was actually buried with, Henettawy's wooden coffins and inner mummy lid were intricate and detailed. Each piece was made to fit into the other like a Russian doll, and elaborate masks are depicted on the heads, shaped like wrapped mummies. This was the new type of coffin of the 21st dynasty—no longer gold, glass, and semiprecious stones. Instead, they are painted with complex symbols and simulations of the lavish coffins of the 18th dynasty. As with Tutankhamen's pendant (*see pages 68–73*) every part is significant. The black wig on Henettawy's face, for instance, symbolizes the fertility of the Nile, while the hair ornaments and wide collar represent the wealth—and so importance—she had during her life.

This is the goddess Ma'at—the goddess of justice and the highest moral authority of Egyptian society. She was usually depicted with an ostrich feather on her head and with wings attached to her arms.

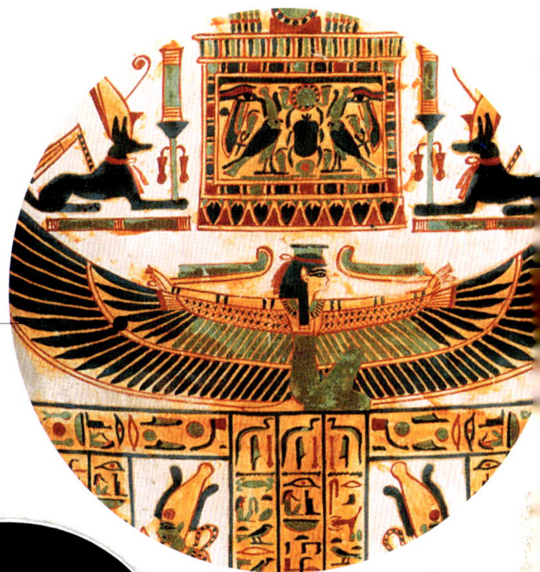

Henettawy's wig and funerary jewelry are typical of the period. The face, arms, and jewelry are idealized instead of realistic, indicating her prosperity and significance.

Pattern and order is unmistakable within this structured design, and rhythms are created by repetitions of images and hieroglyphs. Figures stand out clearly on the white background, and clarity and balance are achieved by thickly applied dark red, green, and black on the yellow background.

The decoration of this piece reflects royal coffins of an earlier age, with their gold and other precious materials. Painted to resemble a mummy itself, richly colored emblems are also painted to look as if they are fastened to the cloth wrappings. Two udjat (or wedjat) eyes, represent the right eye of Horus or it was associated with the Sun God Ra. Believed to have healing and protective power, the eyes appear just below Henettawy's elbows. An elaborate pectoral in the shape of a small shrine sits between the udjat eyes. At the sides are figures of Anubis as a jackal wearing the crowns of Upper and Lower Egypt and holding royal scepters. Nut, the sky goddess, spreads her protective wings and beneath her, vertical and horizontal yellow bands (representing gold) cover the white mummy wrapping.

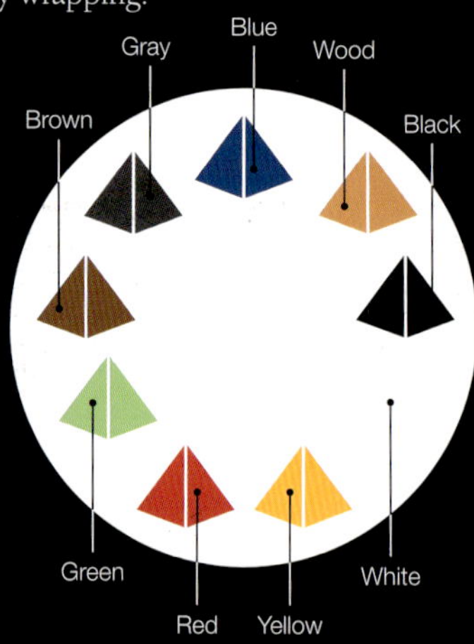

Black, blue, brown, gray, green, red, white, and yellow pigments were mixed with water and viscous materials, such as egg yolk or plant sap, creating tempera.

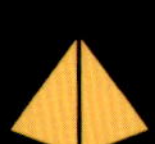

The pigments were still mainly minerals such as copper, chalk, and soot (carbon). The bright yellow-gold was orpiment, imported from Persia.

Yellow bands painted between the images represent reed mats, upon which sit high-status people and other symbols and hieroglyphs signifying "stability" and "perfection."

Constructed from wood and coated with plaster reinforced with thinly woven fine linen, Henettawy's two coffins and mummy board were elaborately painted and varnished. On this, gesso was applied to prepare the wood before applying paint. Gesso was painted on, left to dry, and then the surface was sanded and polished to a smooth finish, leaving it hard and inflexible. The grid was marked on using string dipped in red paint and the images drawn lightly in place. Next, pigments were finely ground, then mixed with water and tree gum and applied in flat areas. Finally, once the paint was completely dry, a colorless resin varnish was painted on, enriching the bright colors with a clear sheen.

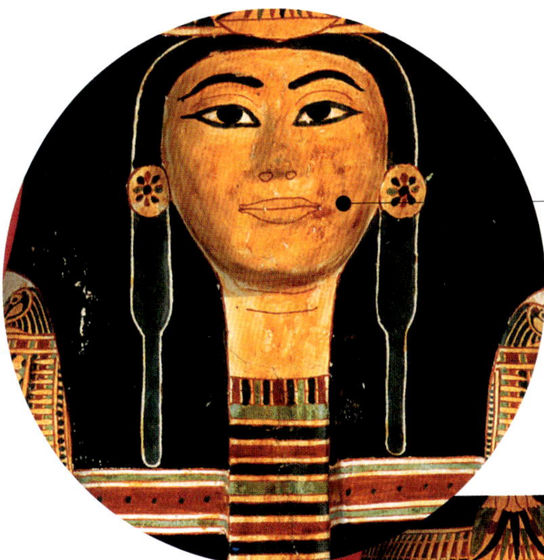

Without the enormous wealth of previous dynasties, artists had to emulate the look of gold and semiprecious stones.

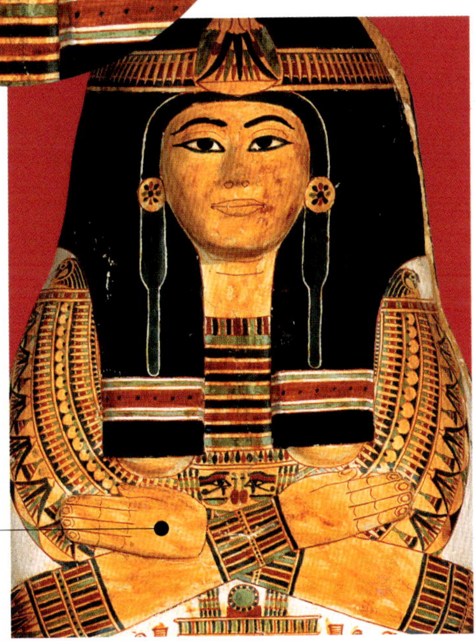

Acacia and sycamore, or cedar from Lebanon provided much of the wood used to make furniture and coffins. Wood carvers had to peg pieces of wood together and used flint, copper, and bronze tools to cut away and shape the wood.

Henettawy's crossed arms echo the conventions of past pharaohs, which lasted throughout the dynasties.

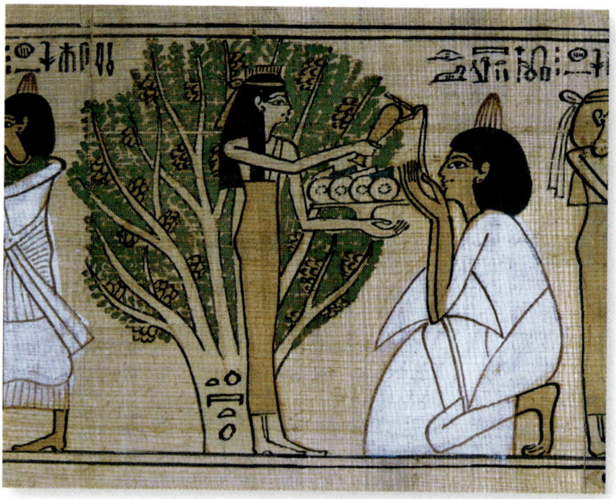

FROM DEIR EL-BAHRI, WESTERN THEBES, NOW IN THE KUNSTHISTORISCHES MUSEUM, VIENNA

Book of the Dead of Khensumose

Paint and ink on papyrus, 1040–991 BCE

IN THE 21ST DYNASTY, Egyptian beliefs still relied on the rituals and acts that led to the gods admitting the dead to the afterlife. Even when the materials and styles changed, this remained the motivating force behind all Egyptian funerary art. It is one of the most conspicuous features of the civilization that continued through the Old, Middle, and New Kingdoms and was just as important during the Third Intermediate Period, although some of the art had changed subtly by then.

Nut was believed to be the goddess of the sky and heavens, associated with both day and night. In later periods, she was no longer just the goddess of the daytime sky, but of the sky and heavens in general. She was the daughter of

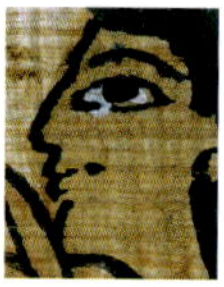

c.1307–1196 BCE

The 19th dynasty sees previously peaceful pharaohs becoming more organized to fight and defend Egypt

c.1196–1070 BCE

Conquests bring new people, fashions, words, and religious cults into Egypt

c.1196–1070 BCE

From the 19th dynasty the people make little progress and originality declines

the gods Shu and Tefnut (roughly described as gods of dryness and moisture in the atmosphere) and the granddaughter of the sun god Ra. Her husband was also her brother, Geb, and she was thought to be the mother of Osiris, Set, Isis, and Nephthys as well as grandmother to Horus. Nut was seen as a friend and protector of the dead. In certain spells in the Book of the Dead she was called on to help the dead pass through the underworld, Duat, to reach the next world. By appearing on this papyrus, she gave extra help to the owner.

During his life in the Third Intermediate Period, Khensumose was the Chief of the Craftsmen and Chief Archivist of the Treasury of the Amun Temple; he was also Overseer of the Goldsmiths' Workshop and Overseer of all Construction Works, so his papyrus is of particular quality and beauty. Consisting mainly of illustrations, it is classed as one of the "Mythological Papyri," which is a term that describes the extra-long scrolls produced in the 21st dynasty around Thebes, with scenes painted either in black or in color, and vignettes following each other from right to left. Many of these scrolls contain funerary compositions and themes different from Books of the Dead made in earlier periods. Khensumose appears in every vignette and all the drawings are elegant and simplified, but the style is slightly different from earlier Egyptian texts and painted in fewer colors.

Fact

Generally, the figures of pharaohs, gods, and goddesses were portrayed in formal style adhering to long-established rules, but lesser mortals, such as Khensumose, were allowed to be interpreted less formally.

6 in (15.5 cm)

13.4 ft (410 cm)

c.1081 BCE

The Story of Wenamun is written—a story about a priest at the Amun Temple who went to buy cedar wood but failed

c.1080–1050 BCE

Foreigners make up much of the workforce, but only Egyptians are admitted into the roles of scribe and priest

1070–945 BCE

Tombs no longer decorated sumptuously, but coffins or papyri are embellished

c.1006 BCE

Possible start of the reign of the Biblical King David, who built the great temple of Jerusalem

This scene was particularly important in the Mythological Papyri because it describes Nut helping Khensumose directly. She is standing in front of her sacred sycamore fig tree, giving Khensumose bread and water to sustain him on his journey to the afterlife. On the tree trunk, the name of the goddess Nut is written in hieroglyphs. Contrary to preceding artistic practice, Khensumose is portrayed larger than the goddess in the picture. Uncommonly too, Nut is in the primary right-facing position and the large figure of Khensumose is in the secondary left-facing one—in most Books of the Dead, the deceased would face right and the god or goddess would face left.

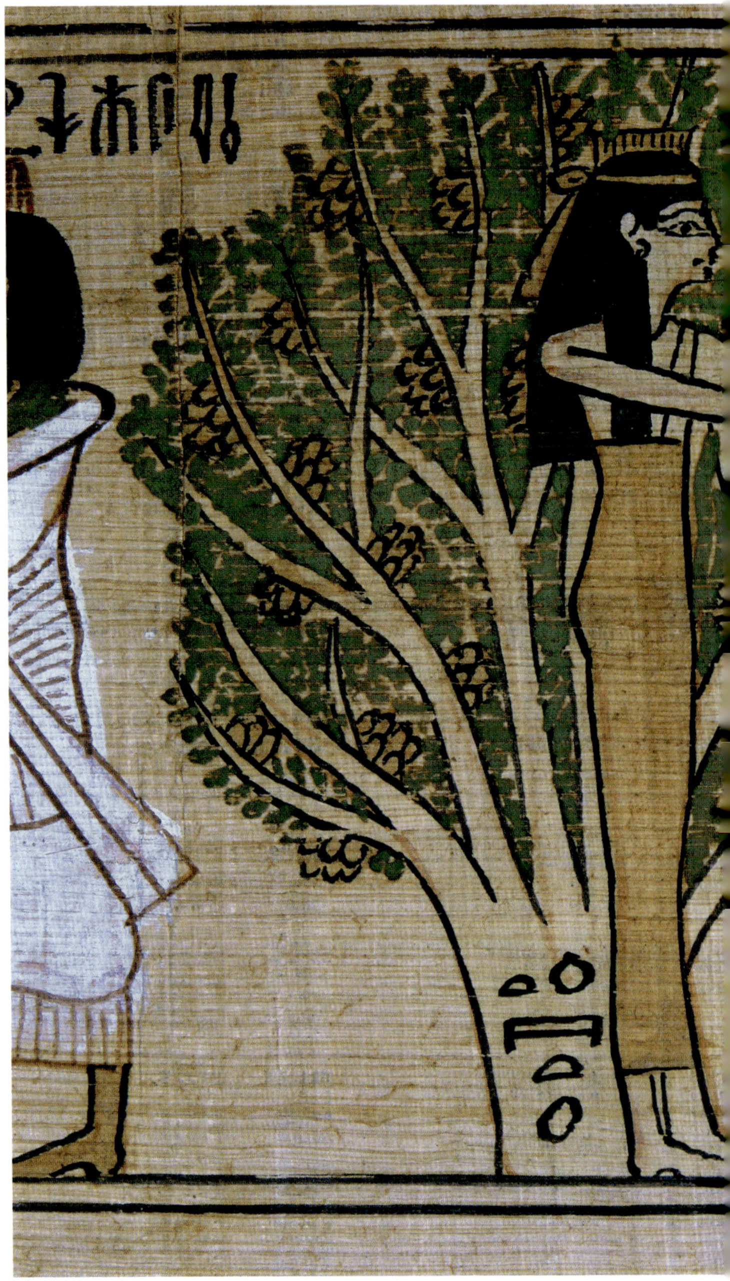

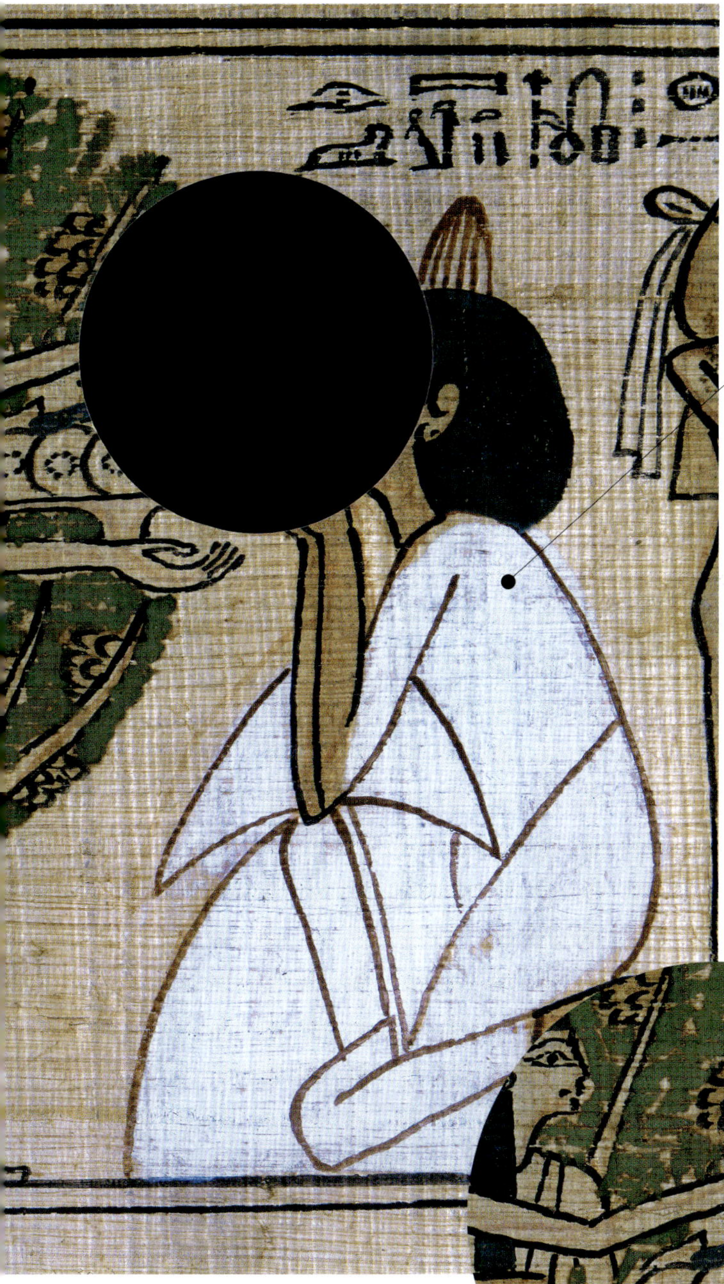

Kneeling before Nut in the garden of earthly paradise, Khensumose receives the water of life and the fruit of the sacred sycamore fig tree.

Nut holds a plate of food in her left hand and gives water to Khensumose from a yellow libation vase in her right hand.

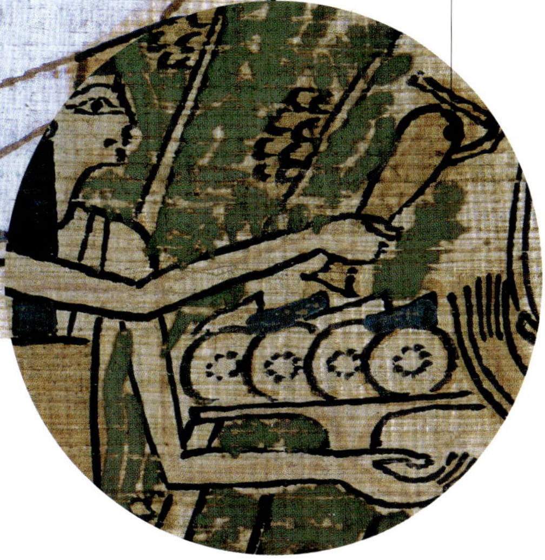

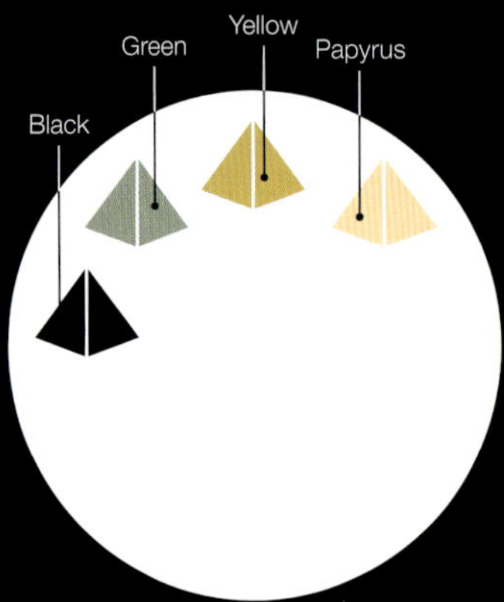

As the Chief of Craftsmen, Khensumose probably designed this papyrus. The color scheme of white, yellow, black, and green is individual and stylish.

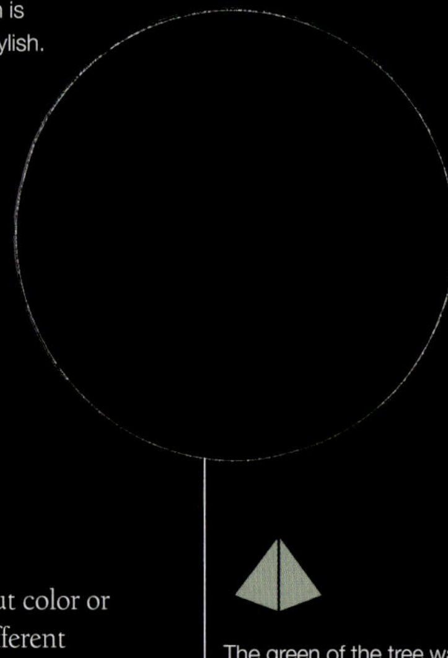

Other Books of the Dead at the time were either without color or with only a little color as here. The images were also different from many of the earlier illustrations and this, although a well-known story, has been illustrated in a new way. Everything is outlined in black and green is the predominant color. Green still symbolized new life, growth, fertility, rebirth, resurrection, and vegetation. It was viewed as a healing color, connected with well-being and flourishing health and according to prevailing beliefs, health was essential in the afterlife.

The green of the tree was the color of growth and of life itself. Green also came to be associated with resurrection through the annual return of green plants. Malachite was used here to make the green color.

This painter was skilled at blending primary colors into subtle shades. The green was most likely copper ore, white was calcium sulfate, black was carbon, and yellow was orpiment. All were mixed with a binding vegetable gum and applied with water.

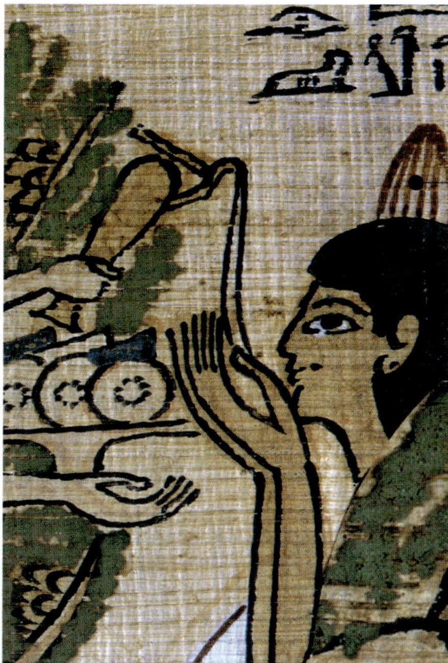

The wax cone was a popular form of pomade worn on top of the head. The cone is usually white with streaks of orange brown running from its top.

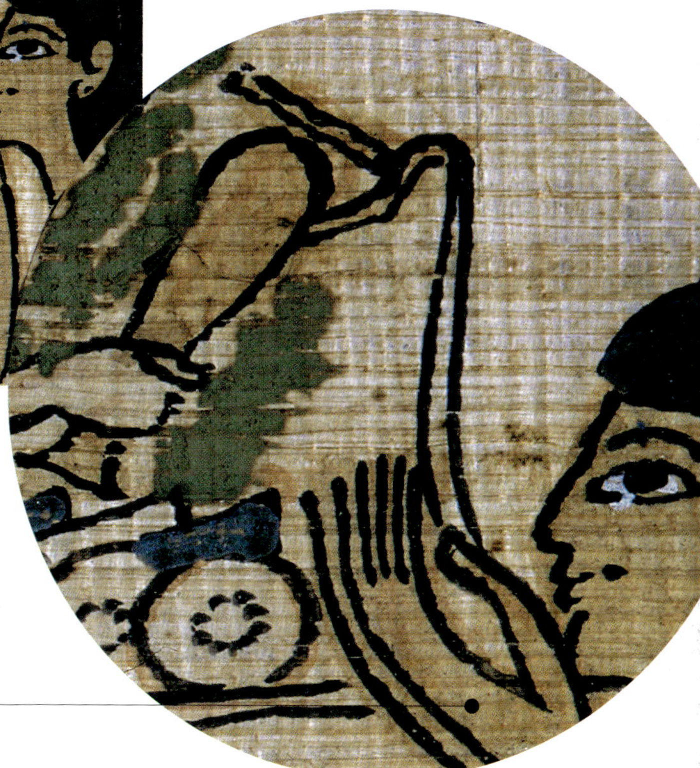

Compare the hands of Khensumose to those on the relief on page 28. Depictions of hand shapes had not changed in nearly four hundred years.

The outline scribe devoted as much time, energy, and skill into his initial drawings as the artists who planned the original composition and painted on the colors. This was not a rushed job. Preliminary outlines reveal a subtlety and elegance of draftsmanship, and professional pride dictated that care and attention to detail was maintained, even if the work was not due to be seen by any living eyes. Although Nut seems to our eyes to be standing in front of the sycamore fig tree, the Egyptians would have accepted that she was in the tree, because they all knew that it was sacred to her and she was often shown standing in a sycamore fig tree pouring either water or wine from a jar.

Compositions like this were team efforts, with the design set by the chief artist and the drawing and painting executed by another skilled artist.

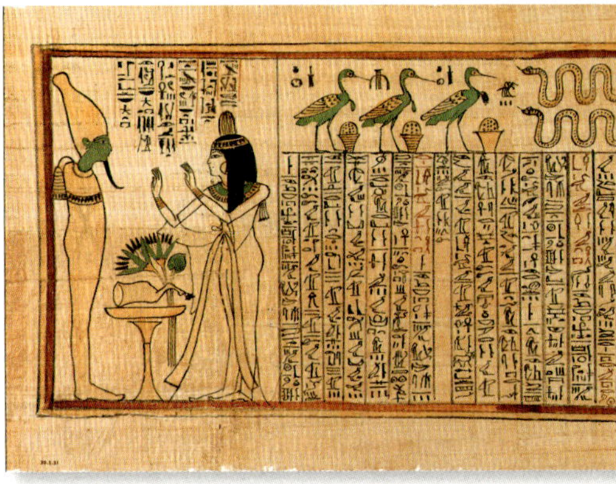

FROM THE TOMB OF NANY, WESTERN THEBES, NOW IN THE METROPOLITAN MUSEUM OF ART, NEW YORK

Section from the Book of the Dead of Nany

Painted and inscribed papyrus, c.1040–945 BCE

WHEN SHE DIED DURING THE 21ST DYNASTY of the Third Intermediate Period, Nany was in her seventies. Like Henettawy (*see pages 104–109*), in life she was a singer (chantress) in the Temple of Amun at Thebes. Nany was also referred to as a "king's daughter," which probably means that she was the daughter of Pinodjem I, the high priest of Amun and effectively the ruler of the country at that time.

As was customary during the period, her coffin and boxes of *shawabtis* (small funerary statuettes, also called *shabtis* or *ushabtis*) were placed in her tomb, close to her coffin, with a hollow wooden Osiris figure containing a papyrus scroll inscribed with a collection of texts from the Book of the Dead. This is part of that papyrus.

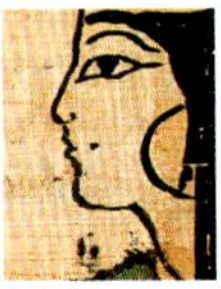

c.1180–1170 BCE

Most of Southern Egypt is under the control of the military

c.1070 BCE

Former Theban High Priest Pinudjem I takes a royal title

c.1070–945 BCE

Many soldier-priests of Thebes are closely related to the Tanis pharaohs

During this period, exceptional attention was paid to burial practices, which had changed somewhat from previous periods. Changes were introduced in methods of mummification and in the actual forms of the burial. Books of the Dead were no longer filled with so many vignettes as in earlier periods and although the drawings are competent and the coloring careful, the images seem unimaginative and do not compare with the remarkable productions of the New Kingdom.

Although there were some restrictions, Nany—like other women of ancient Egypt—enjoyed an unusual level of independence regarding legal and economic rights. Her papyrus was made personally for her, created by a scribe, illustrated by an artist, and would have been expensive. Not many Books of the Dead were made like this for women before this time. Royal or noble men traditionally had them made, but not females. In this vignette, to please Osiris, Nany makes an offering of a leg of beef. Osiris was often depicted with a green face, a mummified human wearing a white crown (a royal symbol), and the curving god's beard. The crown was white with a plume on both sides and a small disk at the top, worn for certain religious rituals. As king of the underworld, Osiris admitted only those who had lived good lives and who had received proper burial rights. If he judged someone worthy, he allowed that person into the idyllic afterlife.

This papyrus is traditionally bordered with brown and yellow and the hieroglyphs are in columns. Red hieroglyphs indicate the beginning of a sentence and the layout clearly follows an orderly grid structure.

Fact

Egyptian artists knew that the intense colors of mineral and synthetic pigments would be unlikely to deteriorate. They were used in wall paintings and on coffins, only probably mixed with different binders for papyrus.

10in (25.7 cm)

13½ in (34.9 cm)

c.1070–940 BCE

Temples built in Tanis, mostly constructed with stone salvaged from the northerly cities

c.1069 BCE

Focus of artistic production changed as vogue for large tombs declined

c.1050 BCE

Exterior and interior decoration of coffins and artifacts exceeds previous lavishness

1040 BCE

Pinudjem's son, Psusennes I, becomes pharaoh in Tanis

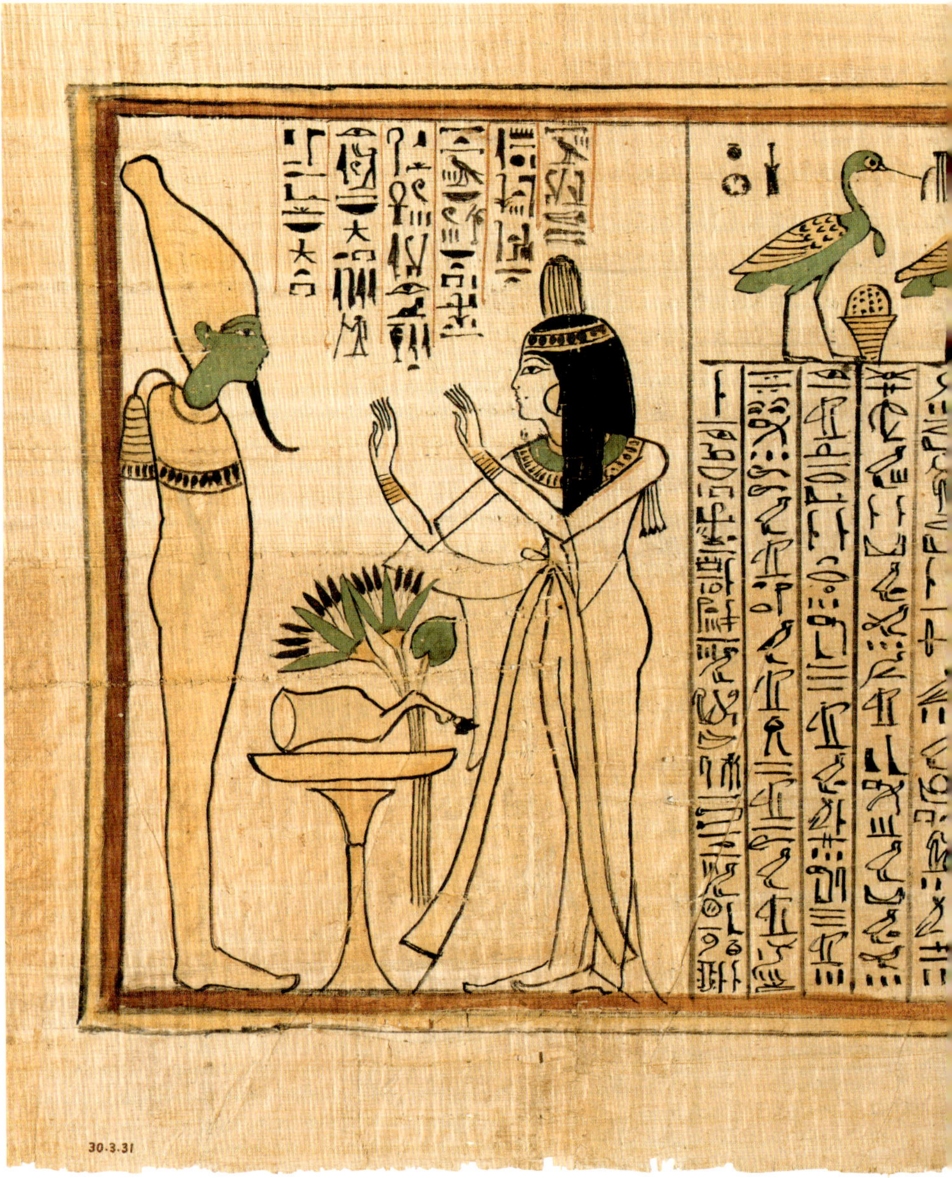

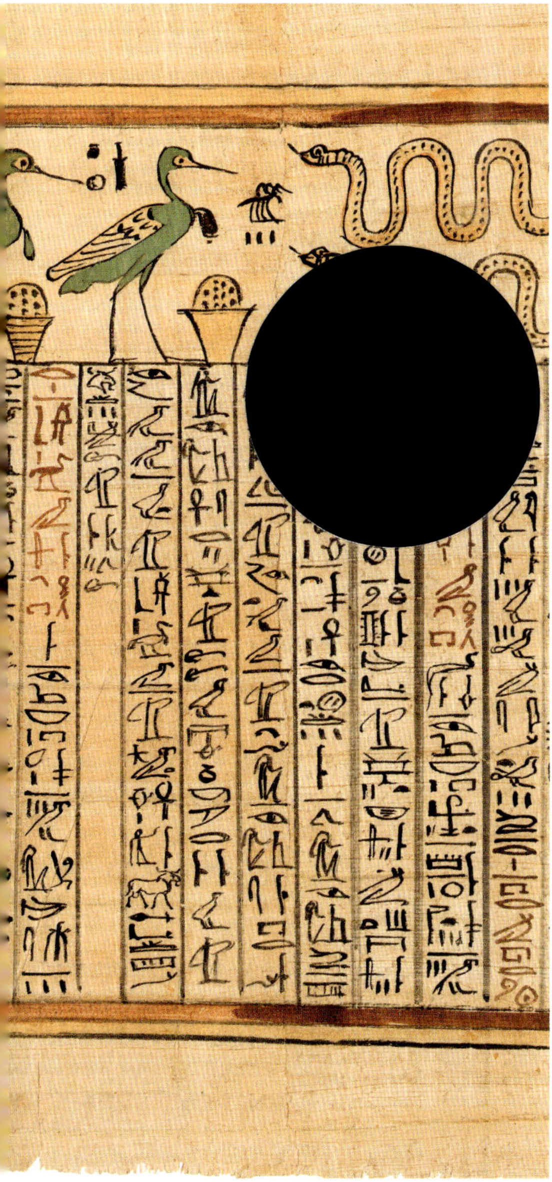

This papyrus with its inscribed symbols and words was believed to have magical power that would protect and provide for Nany in the afterlife. When unrolled, it is more than 17 ft (5 m) long. Since this is the far left side of the papyrus roll, it is the end, because it is read from right to left. This shows the climax of Nany's journey to the afterlife—the moment where Osiris tells her whether or not she can pass through to the next world. Portrayed with a green face, because he was also the god of fertility, resurrection, and power over new vegetation, Osiris is wrapped like a mummy. This was traditional because, as all Egyptians believed, Osiris was originally a beloved pharaoh, murdered by his jealous brother Set, who spread his body across the Nile in 14 pieces. Osiris' wife Isis gathered up her husband's pieces and bandaged them together in linen cloth. With the help of Anubis, the god of the afterlife, and powerful charms, Isis was able to bring Osiris back to life as a god of the next world.

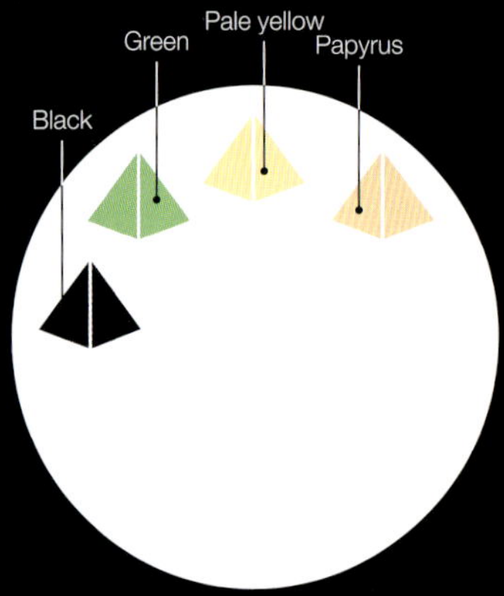

The emphasis on the color green is not accidental. Made with powdered malachite, a natural copper ore from the Sinai and Eastern Deserts, it symbolized fertility and new life.

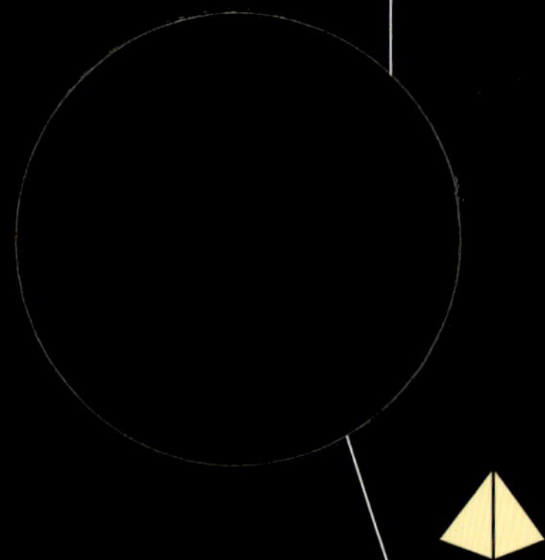

Indicating specialized knowledge of chemistry, the pale yellow is synthetic, either lead white or lead antimonate, made by chemical transformations of minerals.

In Egyptian art, the heron was thought to be the original phoenix—it represented the sun and rebirth. It was also thought to be the Ba (soul) of both Ra and Osiris. The three featured here foretold of good things for Nany. The snakes are probably the goddess Hauhet, who symbolized infinity. Offerings to the gods were made during life to ensure that ancestors continued in their eternal life. Thus, the offering of the joint of beef suggests that Nany is also about to be granted everlasting life. Although this papyrus is heavy with symbolism, as papyri were during previous dynasties, the style is changing. The vignettes are more intermingled with the text and the pictures are less detailed and not so colorful.

The palette of the artist is more subdued in Nany's Book of the Dead than at any time before. This is partly to do with the fashion, partly because of the expense, and partly as a consequence of changes in religious significance.

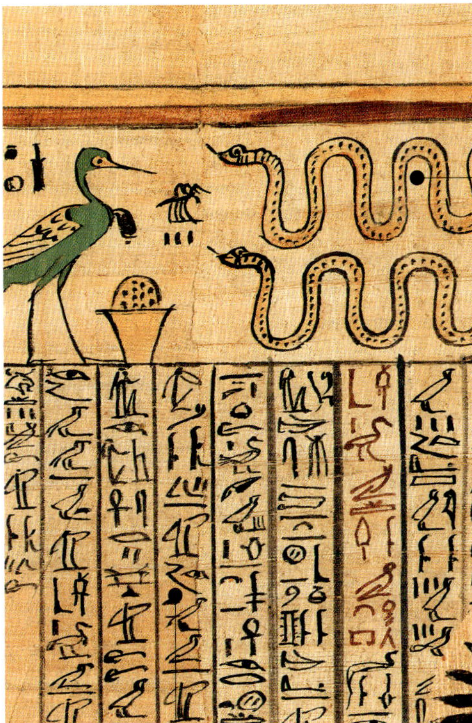

The detailed illustrative images of the vignettes mark the beginning of illuminated manuscripts, which were continued in Christian and Islamic examples.

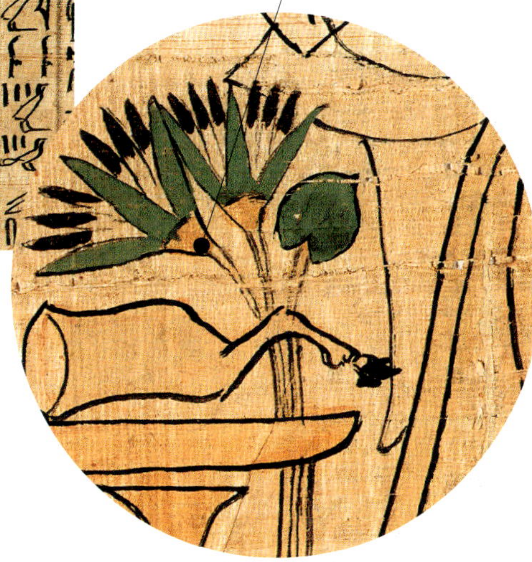

This small still life shows two lotus flowers, which were sweet smelling, and a lily pad next to the offering table laden with beef—the flowers are part of the offering, and/or contribute to the sacred space of the scene.

The hieroglyphs and columns are methodically placed and not packed in around the vignettes as in some earlier papyri. The overall impression, intentionally created, is of space and elegance. As with the necessity for comprehensible images, it was imperative that the hieroglyphs were legible.

The way we perceive an image and the way the Egyptians perceived that same image are fundamentally different. When a person is shown doing something as here, the Egyptians believed that it would happen. So by painting Nany praying to Osiris, Egyptian artists believed that they were making this occur. Legibility was imperative so the artists have continued to make this as clear as possible without worrying about attempting realism. The arms and hands are both left versions and the eye remains front-facing while the face is in profile. The long spindly arms, sash, and transparency of the gown demonstrate the enduring Egyptian philosophies of showing objects from real life in their simplest and most straightforward ways.

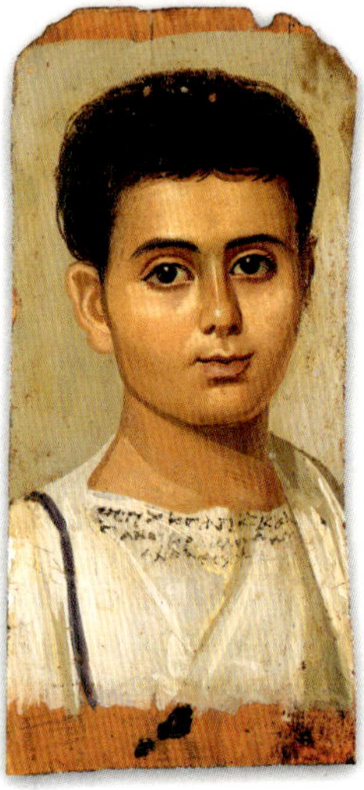

ORIGINALLY FOUND IN THE FAIYUM AREA OF EGYPT, NOW IN THE METROPOLITAN MUSEUM OF ART, NEW YORK

Portrait of a Boy

Encaustic paint on limewood,
Roman Period, 2nd century CE

EGYPT WAS CONQUERED BY ROME AND WAS A PART OF THE Roman Empire between 30 BCE (when Cleopatra died) and 395 CE. This portrait was created during that period. Some of the funeral portraits painted then survived in the dry climate of Egypt but not in Rome and are the only paintings of the Roman period that have lasted, apart from some frescoes on interior walls. This particular portrait is believed to have come from Antinoopolis, a Roman-controlled city on the east bank of the Nile. The portrait's function was as a mask secured over the face of the dead by linen mummy bandages.

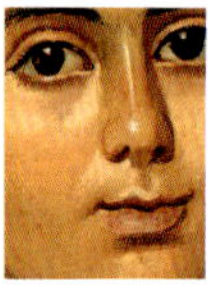

332 BCE

Alexander III of Macedon (Alexander the Great) defeats the Persians, assisting the Egyptians considerably

30 BCE

Conquest of Egypt by Octavian, later known as Emperor Augustus, following defeat of Mark Antony and Cleopatra

c.20 BCE

Roman emperors represent themselves as the successors to the pharaohs and continue to build temples in Egyptian style

All portraits of this type are believed to have been painted from living models, and were possibly even displayed during life, although the paintings were also used in funeral practices, tied onto the deceased's mummy. The skillful rendering of this boy's features was intended to preserve his appearance for the afterlife in the same sentiment as with earlier Egyptian painting but, while the belief may have been the same, the execution is very different from earlier Egyptian art.

The art of the portrait flourished in Greek and Roman art, where sitters demanded realistic images, even unflattering ones. This was painted when naturalism was still in favor and shows a degree of realism that had not been attempted before in Egypt. This style of painting, so different from the traditional Egyptian style but well known in Greco-Roman Egypt, originated in Classical Greece in the 5th and 4th centuries BCE.

The inscription in dark purple pigment below the neckline of the boy's tunic identifies the dead boy, and reveals some interesting information about his short life: "Eutyches, the freed slave of Kasanios. I, Heraclides, son of Evander, have countersigned." Slavery was widespread in the Greek and Roman world. Some slaves, like Eutyches, were raised in their masters' homes from birth, forming close relationships. A master could grant freedom to a favorite slave, as Kasianos did for young Eutyches. This new status was important in both life and death. This mummy portrait was probably also paid for by Eutyches' former master, Kasianos.

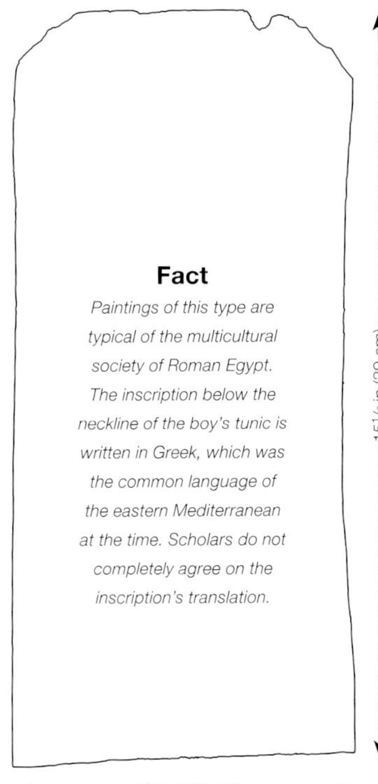

Fact

Paintings of this type are typical of the multicultural society of Roman Egypt. The inscription below the neckline of the boy's tunic is written in Greek, which was the common language of the eastern Mediterranean at the time. Scholars do not completely agree on the inscription's translation.

c.5 CE

Birth of Jesus Christ in Bethlehem

c.1–300 CE

The Ancient Egyptian funerary tradition continues, but art evolves with the incorporation of Greco-Roman techniques and styles

c.138–161 CE

Last major Roman temples are constructed in the traditional pharaonic style

189–222 CE

Bishop Demetrius spends time in Egypt, converting many to Christianity

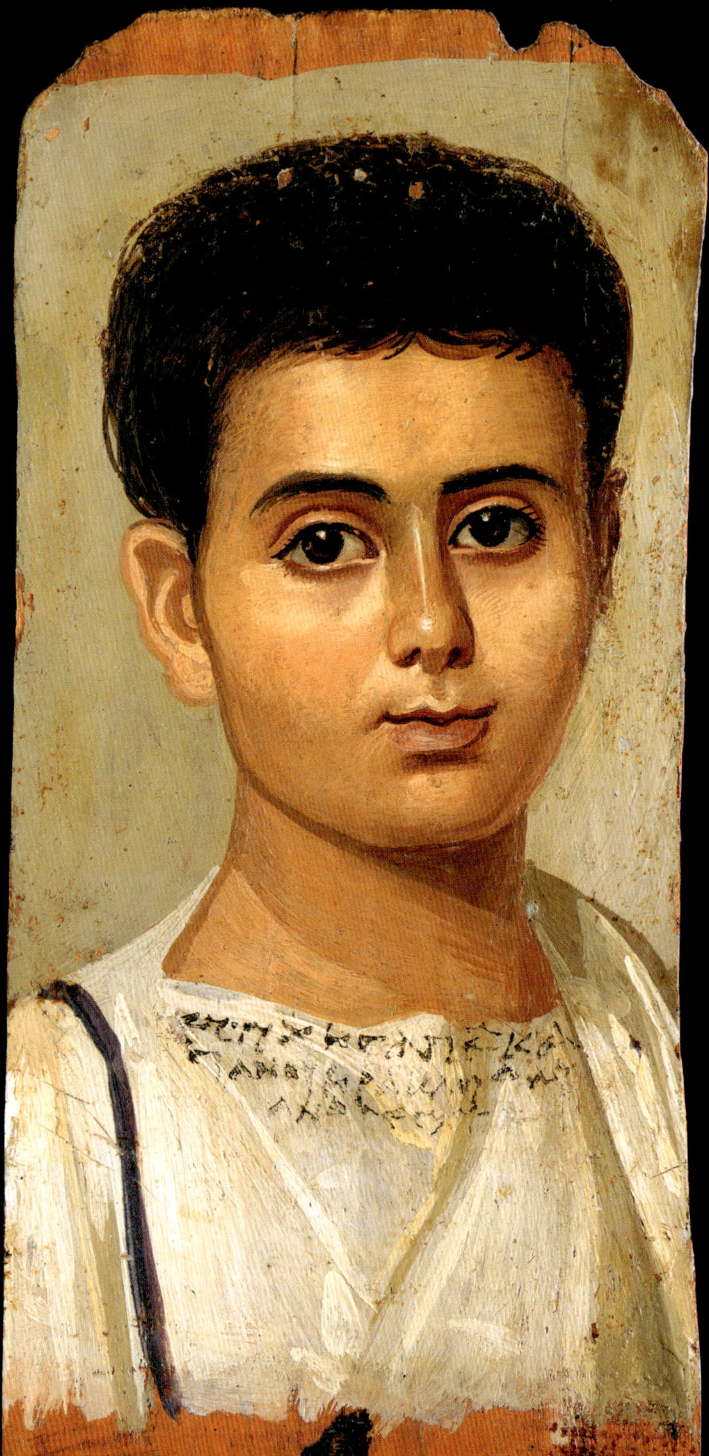

The young teenage boy looks calmly at the viewer, his head at an almost three-quarter angle. Dressed in a white Roman tunic, he has a narrow purple clavus (a vertical stripe) over his right shoulder. A cloak of the same color as the tunic is draped over his left shoulder. His short dark hair is brushed back behind his ears and his features are natural and relaxed. He was probably about 14 years old when this was painted. Although the brush marks are somewhat visible, the entire image is extremely realistically conveyed, particularly when compared with traditional Egyptian art. The upper right edge of the panel is damaged and there are marks where the mummy bands were wrapped around the painting.

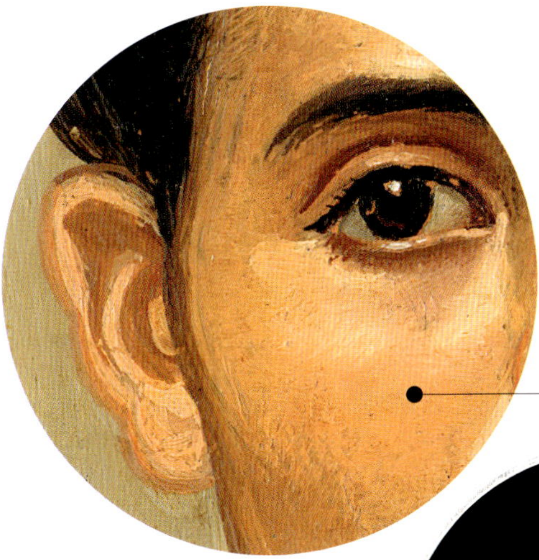

Whereas previous Egyptian paintings had depicted faces in profile with eyes facing, this is a sophisticated viewpoint—later emulated by Renaissance artists.

Although not royal, this boy was part of a privileged class. The painter worked quickly, rendering the smooth tones of the skin and the intense gaze but, conforming to convention, he did not try to capture any facial expression or emotion.

The face has highlights on the nose and forehead as well as shadows under the chin, creating an impression of solid, three-dimensionality.

Illusionistic painting tries to create three-dimensional space on a two-dimensional surface, whereas traditional Egyptian art has no interest in depicting depth and space on a two-dimensional surface. Here, the boy's head gives the impression of depth, standing out from the light olive-colored background. His face is modeled with long brushstrokes and a subtle blend of light and dark colors. Shadows on the left side of the face, neck, and garment, and white highlights on the forehead and below the right eye indicate a strong source of light from the right. The portrait was painted using the elaborate encaustic technique, using pigments mixed with hot beeswax and, in some parts, other ingredients such as egg, resin, and linseed oil. The artist probably applied a uniform flesh tone, coarsely blended, all over the facial area, then blended in the darks and lights.

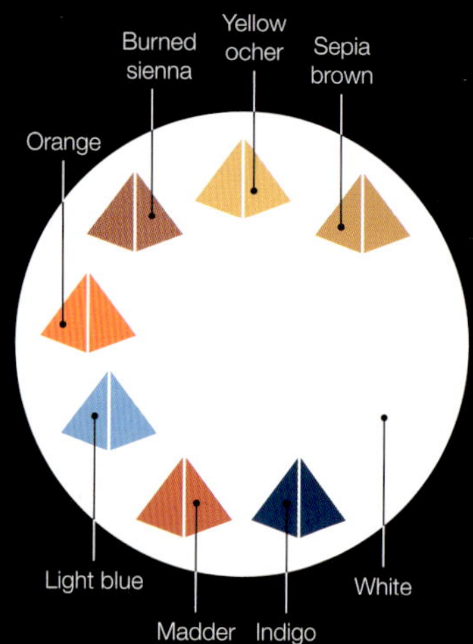

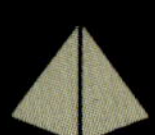

Although a certain amount of fading has probably occurred, the pale olive-green background was intentionally bland, almost as a foil for the face.

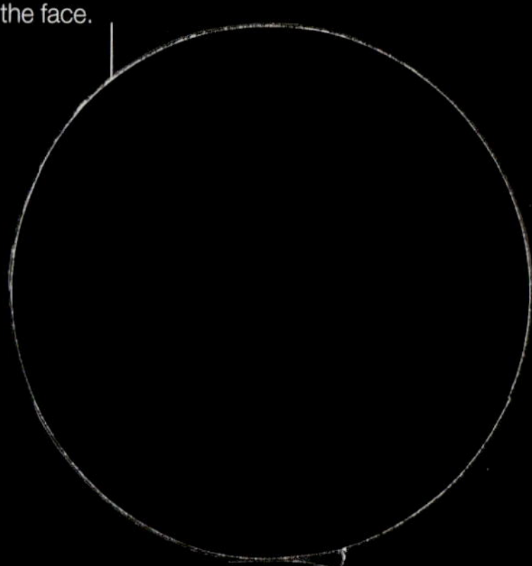

The eyes are painted with darkest sepia brown around black pupils that reflect the light with bright spots of white.

The pigments used were similar to those used in earlier periods. They included: lime sulfate (white), yellow ocher, rose madder, iron oxide (burned sienna), charcoal, lead oxide (orange), and copper (light blue) Madder lake, a dark reddish-purple color that could be mixed with indigo to make violet. Both pigments came from plant roots.

Beginning with a thin, rectangular piece of polished limewood, the portrait outline was lightly drawn onto the wood with charcoal before being painted. Next, beeswax was blended over heat with tree resin for hardness when it dried and sometimes linseed oil for fluidity. Once this mixture was molten, the dry colored pigments were added and then quickly painted onto the wooden support using natural hair brushes. Lingering would lead to the wax solidifying on the brush. Heated metal tools and special brushes were used to shape the paint before it solidified and to manipulate the wax once it had cooled on the surface. This method of painting, known as encaustic, had a similar appearance to oil painting of later centuries.

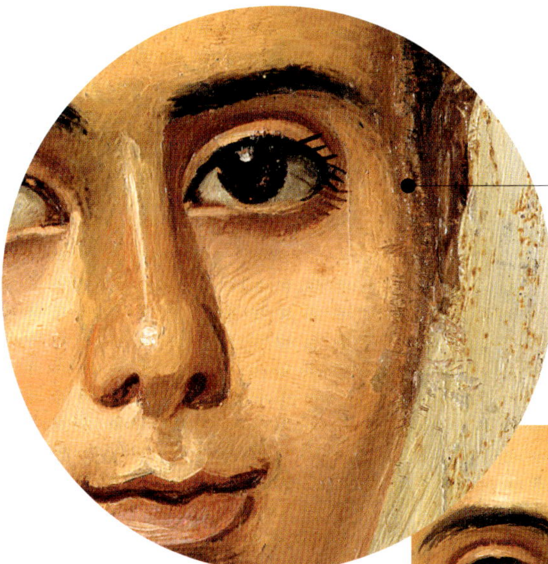

For the first time in history, artists painted from direct observation, trying to render their subject with vivid and realistic accuracy.

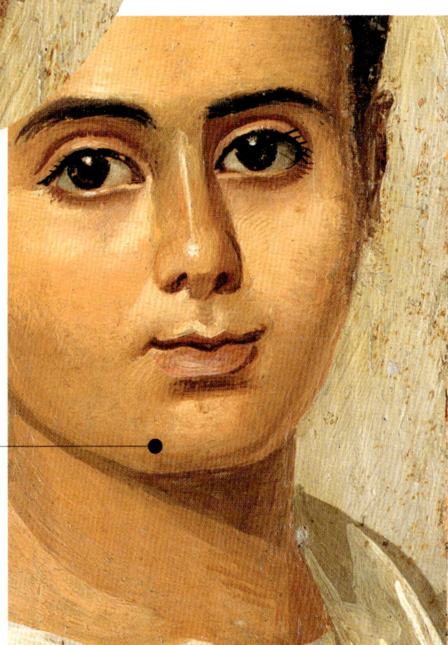

The face has highlights on the nose and forehead as well as shadows under the chin, creating an impression of solid, three-dimensionality.

Parts of the portrait were painted with cool wax that was kept malleable by being emulsified with egg and then applied with brushes.

Index